Women and the Shaping of Catholicism

Women Through the Ages

A Symposium With
Richard W. Miller, PhD, Susan A. Calef, PhD,
William Harmless, SJ, PhD, Gary Macy, PhD,
Eileen C. Burke-Sullivan, STD, Robert Ellsberg,
Mary Ann Zimmer, ND, PhD

Edited by Richard W. Miller

Liguori
LIGUORI, MISSOURI

Imprimi Potest:
Thomas D. Picton, C.Ss.R.
Provincial, Denver Province,
The Redemptorists

Library of Congress Cataloging-in-Publication Data
Women and the shaping of Catholicism : women through the ages / edited
by Richard W. Miller.
    p. cm.
Conference proceedings.
ISBN 978-0-7648-1770-0
    1. Catholic women--History--Congresses. 2. Women in the Catholic
Church--History--Congresses. I. Miller, Richard W.
    BX4667.W66 2009
    282.082--dc22

                                                              2008045019

Published by Liguori Publications
Liguori, Missouri 63057-9999

Liguori Publications, a nonprofit corporation, is an apostolate of the Redemptorists. To learn more about the Redemptorists, visit Redemptorists.com.

To order, call 800-325-9521.
www.liguori.org

Printed in the United States of America
13 12 11 10 09 5 4 3 2 1

Contents

Introduction

Richard W. Miller, PhD, Assistant Professor of Systematic Theology
Creighton University

This year's conference draws on the expertise of distinguished American theologians to consider the remarkably diverse ways that women have had a profound influence on the Catholic community and world from the time of Christ to the present day. The conference will not only explore the ways women religious have shaped Catholicism at certain points in its history, but will also examine the impact of laywomen in the history of Catholicism.

The first paper, *Hearing Women's Voices*, which is my contribution, describes the pervasiveness of androcentrism in the history of Western culture and the Christian community. It presents theological grounds for the particular focus of the day; namely, hearing women's voices throughout the tradition. Furthermore, it argues that the topic for the day is not just a women's issue but an urgent question for the whole community.

The second through seventh papers are organized according to the various epochs of the Christian tradition and treat various issues and figures in these periods. The second paper, by Susan Calef, treats *Women in the New Testament*. Dr. Calef's paper focuses on the two earliest generations of Christian women, namely, those around Jesus in his reign of God movement and those in the Pauline mission field. Among the questions she addresses: What was the status of women in the Jesus movement? Were women among Jesus' disciples? Were any of them apostles? What do we know about the roles and contributions of women in Pauline communities? In pursuing these questions, she will focus attention on four women: Mary Magdalene, Phoebe, Junia, and Prisca.

The third paper, by William Harmless, is called *Women in the Early Church: A Portrait Gallery*. Fr. Harmless surveys the extraordinary and wide-ranging contributions of Christian women during the patristic era (100–600). He surveys both a range of figures (e.g., Thecla, Perpetua, Proba, Egeria, Melania the Elder, Olympias) and their remarkable contributions as apostles, martyrs, poets, pilgrims, patrons, deaconesses, and monks.

The fourth paper, by Gary Macy, is on *Women of the Middle Ages*. Dr. Macy presents evidence that women in the Middle Ages played a far larger role in the life of the Church than they would in later centuries. In the early

Middle Ages, they performed sacramental and administrative functions that would be reserved for men after the thirteenth century. They celebrated Mass, distributed Communion, read the Gospel, heard confessions, and preached. Some abbesses also exercised episcopal power and, indeed, a few were considered bishops. The powerful Abbess of Las Huelgas in Spain continued to wear her mitre and exercise administrative episcopal power until 1874.

The fifth paper, by Eileen Burke-Sullivan, is on *Women of the Catholic Reformation and Early Modern Period.* Dr. Burke-Sullivan shows how women in this period achieved some small measure of personal autonomy but at the very high price of the death of thousands of women through the demented witchcraft craze that swept Europe and the New Worlds. Her paper focuses on how Teresa of Avila, Isabella of Castile, Mary Ward of England, and Leonor Mascarenhas and her daughter Leonor de Vega Osorio contributed to striking changes in the practice of faith and the structural life of the Church and culture.

The sixth paper, by Robert Ellsberg, is on *Catholic Women in the Nineteenth and Twentieth Centuries.* Through the example of women saints, he highlights the struggle of women to discern their vocation in ways that challenged the roles and expectation of the day. He looks at the shift from a concept of religious life focused on the cloister to one engaged in the world and the challenges of ordinary life. He treats two nineteenth-century nuns, Anne-Marie Javouhey and Mother Theodore Guerin and examines the extraordinary struggles of Cornelia Connelly, founder of the Society of the Holy Child Jesus. Finally, he shows how the spirituality of Thérèse of Lisieux informed the practice of two twentieth-century lay Christians, Madeline Delbrêl and Dorothy Day.

The seventh paper, by Mary Ann Zimmer, is called *Which Mary, Which Woman, Which Church?* Sr. Zimmer argues that Mary has had such varied and multiple roles in influencing both women and the Church that an attempt to assess her impact can profitably begin by asking those questions. Her paper uses Laura Leming's understanding of "religious agency" to examine when and how varied understandings of Mary have acted upon and with women to shape the Church.

These papers and the lively panel discussion that follows intend to help readers become more critically aware of the destructiveness of the androcentrism that has informed Western culture and the Christian community, while bringing to their attention the extraordinary ways women worked in and around these inhibiting culture structures to further the mission of the Church. The hope is that these papers will in some way further the conversation within the Christian community concerning women and increase the community's commitment to recognizing the full humanity of women and work for their full participation in all aspects of the community's life.

1. Hearing Women's Voices

Richard W. Miller, PhD, Assistant Professor of Systematic Theology
Creighton University

There is something odd about doing a conference on "Women and the Shaping of Catholicism." After all, we are not speaking about something alien or foreign to our experience as a Christian community. The rite of baptism for children in the Roman rite in one of the prayers over the parents recognizes the parents as the first teachers in the ways of faith and encourages them to be the best teachers. The first teachers of children in the faith are not the pope, bishops, priests, or deacons, but the parents. Since the mother has traditionally been the principal caregiver, the mother has been the one primarily involved in educating the children in the faith.

Most of the people in this room have been educated in the faith and also in reading, writing, and arithmetic by women religious; many have been cared for in hospitals run by women religious, and most of us have participated in liturgical celebrations prepared by women religious and increasingly by women lay ministers. Indeed, parish life in the United States is becoming increasingly dominated by the influence of women: roughly 80 percent of the 31,000 lay ecclesial ministers working in Catholic parishes in the United States are women, with 64 percent lay women and 16 percent women religious.[1] Their ministry includes everything that Matthew 25 suggests is necessary to participate in God's eternal life: they feed the hungry, give drink to the thirsty, take the stranger in, clothe the naked, and visit the sick and imprisoned (31–46). They even sponsor theological conferences, which is oddly missing from the criterion for judgment in Matthew 25.

Women in their ministry throughout the centuries of Christian communal life have given themselves in service to others and, as such, have participated in God's life, for God is love. While God has offered women full participation in God's life, the people of God and their leadership have not offered women full participation in all aspects of the community's life.

While it could be argued that up until the end of the twentieth century, there were more opportunities within the Christian community for women to assume positions of power and authority than in the wider culture,[2] the overall cultural atmosphere within the Church did not recognize the full human dignity of women. The Church shared the same androcentric (male-centered) system of values and symbols as society. In this androcentric system that has dominated Western culture, women have not, with few exceptions, been given equal access to the public sphere.

While women in roughly the first hundred years of Christian life were *relatively* active in the public sphere, Christianity has been under the shadow of an androcentric culture. For most of Christian history, women were considered inferior to men by nature and temperament. Though this is a complicated story, let me just make a few soundings in the history of thought to give us a sense of the scope of the problem. Androcentrism was not part of the message of Christ; nevertheless, Christianity would come to reflect the androcentrism of the culture in which it emerged.

This male-dominated cultural outlook was informed by many sources: the patriarchal culture of the Old Testament and some pagan literature, philosophy, and medicine. According to Elizabeth Clark, traditional attitudes toward women came from "attitudes derived from the Old Testament's adulation of the busy housewife and warnings against 'loose women,' pagan antiquity's ideal of the chaste and retiring matron, and the unfavorable representations of women in some classical literature, especially satire."[3] In addition, the views of Greek philosophers and physicians like Aristotle and later Galen and Aretaeus of Cappadocia contributed to negative views concerning women. Let me just give Aristotle's position, although one would find similar accounts in Galen and Aretaeus of Cappadocia.[4] While knowledge of Aristotle's ideas among the Fathers of the Church was secondhand and not always very accurate, Aristotle's ideas on the inferiority of women were part of the cultural background that would inform early Christianity and would become authoritative in the high middle ages.

Aristotle's view that women are inferior was based on his understanding of physiology, which was argued from the dissection of pregnant animals. In Aristotle's physiology, when nature is acting effectively it produces a male, when the agent cause is impaired in some way, it produces a female. Thus in Aristotle's understanding of human conception, a woman is a mistake.[5] She is smaller and weaker, and she is less capable than males of self-control, reason, and virtue. A slight indicator of the insufficiency of Aristotle's science, by our standards, is that one of the ways the agent cause can be thwarted is by the moisture of the south wind.[6] On Aristotelian analysis, we should then expect, in light of our recent rainy weather, that all children conceived in the month of June in the Midwest will be girls.

The conclusion of Aristotle that women were inferior by nature was also held by the second-century philosophers and physicians Galen and

Aretaeus of Cappadocia and would be reiterated by some of the Fathers of the Church. The Eastern Church Father, Clement of Alexandria (150–215), echoes Aristotle's conclusion when he states, "A woman considering what her nature is, must be ashamed of it."[7] Such a view also pervaded the Western Church. In Tertullian (circa 160–225), whose rhetoric was so harsh, we really have a case not only of androcentrism, but misogyny, which is a real hatred of women. Tertullian interpreted the third chapter of Genesis as a story of sexual temptation in which Eve, who represented all women, was the temptress. Tertullian's reading of Genesis 3 leads him to condemn all women in the following passage:

God's judgment on this sex lives on in our age; the guilt necessarily lives on as well. You are the Devil's gateway; you are the unsealer of that tree; you are the first forsaker of the divine law; you are the one who persuaded him whom the Devil was not brave enough to approach; you so lightly crushed the image of God, the man Adam; because of your punishment, that is, death, even the Son of God had to die.[8]

For Tertullian, women were not created in the image of God, as is stated in Genesis 1, but they were responsible for the first sin and by consequence destroyed the image of God in Adam, caused the entrance of death into the world, and thus caused the death of the Son of God.

Women, however, didn't receive only blame in the Patristic period. Indeed, women martyrs and ascetics were extravagantly praised by some of the Fathers of the Church. Listen to Jerome's eulogy of the Roman widow Marcella:

Marcella fasted in moderation, abstained from eating meat, and knew the smell of wine more than its taste, taking it for the sake of her stomach and for her frequent sicknesses (see 1 Timothy 5:23). She rarely used to go out in public and scrupulously shunned the houses of noble ladies, lest she be forced to see that which she had disdained. She frequently visited the basilicas of the apostles and martyrs for private prayers, and avoided the crowded assemblies of the people.... What virtue I found in her, what cleverness, what holiness, what purity, I am afraid to say, lest I exceed what belief finds credible and excite you to greater grief by calling to mind of how great a good you have been deprived.[9]

Such lavish praise, however, did not undermine the androcentrism of the culture; rather, the achievement of these women was explained in andro-centric terms. These women ascetics and martyrs were lauded in the highest terms of their culture—they were seen to have overcome the weakness of their nature such that they had become like men. As Jerome, who had many female friends with whom he investigated Scripture, put it, "she will cease to be a woman and will be called a man."[10]

While Aristotle's view was part of the cultural heritage that informed early Christianity, Aristotle was explicitly cited as an authority in the high middle ages. Thus Thomas Aquinas, when treating the question of the creation of "woman," cites Aristotle. Thomas repeats Aristotle's position when he says, "In respect to the individual nature a woman is defective and a mistake."[11]

Whether we laugh at the absurdity of such statements—and they can be multiplied in different contexts throughout Christian history—or cry at the injustice of them, it is important to recognize, in this case at least, that Thomas was relying on the preeminent authority on these issues of his time: Aristotle. In these matters, Aristotle had the same authority in Thomas's time that the American Medical Association has in our time. Thomas did not question Aristotle as an authority on this issue. Indeed, in the context from which I have taken this text, the received view of Aristotle's poses problems for Thomas's theology. Instead of calling into question Aristotle's view of conception, Thomas accepted it and had to exercise his considerable theologi-cal talent to try to reconcile Aristotle's view that women are a mistake with the Genesis account that "woman" was created in the beginning by God and thus was integral to God's plan in creating.

In showing how Thomas was dependent on Aristotle as the preeminent authority of his time, I have let Thomas off the hook. Thomas was not aware of the evils of androcentrism. He did not know that androcentrism was against God's intent, thus his androcentrism was not sinful. It is only fair to read Thomas in the context of his time. We cannot judge him by the knowledge we have today. We cannot blame Thomas for not being seven hundred years ahead of his time. But in letting Thomas off the hook, have I not downplayed the serious destructiveness and injustice of androcentrism? No, absolutely not. That androcentrism was such part and parcel of Thomas's culture that Thomas did not even question it heightens the seriousness of the problem. It is important to remember that Thomas was not shy about asking questions. Indeed, his *Summa Theologiae*, the masterwork of his over fifty works, has some ten thousand questions, articles, and arguments. That one of the great questioners in the history of Western thought did not see the destructiveness of androcentrism should raise a red flag for us. It calls us to a greater vigilance to bring into the open dehumanizing structures that inform our culture and Christian community.

Women have advanced considerably in the United States since they were given the right to vote in 1920. This is clear from the fact that women have held some of the highest offices in the U.S. government—three of the last four Secretaries of State have been women, the current speaker of the house is a woman, a woman very nearly was the Democratic nominee for president, and women hold 16 percent of the seats in the U.S. House and Senate.[12] Even though great progress has been made in the past hundred years and no major intellectual writing today says women are inferior by nature, sexism is still operative in more subtle ways, and it is imperative to bring it to light. The 1995 United Nations world conference on women states the problem starkly:

> *While women have made significant advances in many societies, women's concerns are still given second priority almost everywhere. Women face discrimination and marginalization in subtle as well as in flagrant ways. Women do not share equally in the fruits of production. Women constitute 70 percent of the world's poor.... Women and men still live in an unequal world. Gender disparities and unacceptable inequalities persist in all countries. In 1995 there is no country in the world where men and women enjoy complete equality.*[13]

This is evidenced not only in the wider society and the world, but also in the Catholic Church. There are a host of instances within the Church. While I cannot mention all of them here, let me just mention a few. According to a 2007 study by the AFL-CIO, jobs in which women represent 70 percent of the workforce pay 30 percent less than jobs that require comparable skills but in which men are more likely employed.[14] Lay ecclesial ministry fits this description, with women employed in 80 percent of the lay ecclesial ministry jobs in the United States.[15] The Catholic community in its support of a just wage needs to counter this gender-based discrimination.

The Catholic community also needs to pay attention to the kind of benefits and services it provides concerning maternal leave. In a survey of women in leadership positions in dioceses across the country, women cited as a major concern family-friendly policies concerning maternal leave that went beyond legal requirements.[16] An example from my own experience, which I have corroborated with other women working in dioceses across the country, can illuminate the problem. When I was a graduate student at Boston

College, my wife, Mariana, was a campus minister at Boston University. Her employer was not Boston University, however, but the Archdiocese of Boston. When she had our first son, the archdiocese gave her unpaid maternity leave for the minimum time required by law. Had she been working in the corporate world, she would have had paid maternity leave. Such a position is not only unjust, but it also flies in the face of the Church's pro life and pro-family commitment.

Finally, and what I find truly scandalous, is the lack of support for women-religious communities as these communities age and lack the finances to provide a humane retirement.

In his 1963 encyclical Peace on Earth (*Pacem in Terris*) Pope John XXIII acknowledged and applauded the shift toward recognizing the full humanity of women that began in the late nineteenth century. He said,

> *It is obvious to everyone that women are now taking a part in public life. This is happening more rapidly perhaps in nations of Christian civilization, and, more slowly but broadly, among peoples who have inherited other traditions or cultures. Since women are becoming ever more conscious of their human dignity, they will not tolerate being treated as mere material instruments, but demand rights befitting a human person both in domestic and public life.*[17]

Women are indeed correctly demanding rights befitting a human person both in domestic and public life. Demanding such rights, however, is not only the obligation of women, but of all of us. Women's inequality in society and the Church is not simply a women's issue, it is an issue for all of us. This is particularly true of the Christian community called to share in God's life.

Why is addressing the inequality of women an issue for the whole Catholic Christian community? I would like in the remaining part of this paper to treat this question theologically. In doing so, I would like to put the subject and the particular focus of this conference on the deepest theological foundation.

God created the universe so human beings could share in God's eternal life. God did not create us out of need. God does not need the universe in order to be God. God in creating does not simply bring into existence beings other than God's self; rather, God brings them into existence so they may share in God's life; so they may enter into fellowship with each other and union with Father, Son, and Holy Spirit. In calling us to friendship and union with God, God is calling us to a union that, according to John Wright, "resembles as far as possible the union between the divine persons themselves."[18] Father, Son, and Holy Spirit are intrinsically and perfectly related to each other in the unity of one nature.[19] The divine persons, according to Wright, "are not only subjectivity, but intersubjectivity within the simple unity of one divine nature."[20]

Human persons, on the other hand, have a natural desire and capacity for intersubjectivity.[21] If all creatures come from God and are oriented toward God as their ultimate fulfillment, then these creatures, because they have a common end, are not only in an ordered relation to God as their end, but are also in an ordered relation to each other. Indeed, the English word *universe* expresses this ordered relation of beings to each other. *Universe* comes from the Latin word *universum*, which literally means "turned toward unity." We are by nature turned toward each other; we are relational by nature. The very orientation of our being is toward unity or community. The perfection of this orientation is only realized through our free act of love. While we are created as oriented by nature toward God and toward each other, it is only by accepting God's call to give of ourselves in love that this natural orientation toward each other and toward God is perfected. As John Wright maintains, "charity or agapē is the principal dynamic force that leads to the fulfillment of God's purposes; for charity both links individuals to the end and unites them to one another in a single community or fellowship in the Holy Spirit."[22]

What these theological reflections demonstrate is that the task of embracing the full humanity of women is not just a women's issue; it is an issue for all of us. If I do not embrace the full humanity of women, I as a man dehumanize myself. I implicitly reject my full humanity and diminish the community of those who love God. I deform the body of Christ.

Part of the task of love is to expose injustice. You cannot work for the justice of the other without naming the injustice done her or him. There is great work to be done in the various disciplines to unmask the social, economic, legal, and educational injustice of androcentrism in Western culture. That is an important task, but not our primary task today. Our task today is to try to listen to women's voices and experiences to the degree that they can be historically reconstructed. According to Irish philosopher and novelist Iris Murdoch, "Love is the difficult realization that something other than oneself is real."[23] To recognize you as real, I must listen to you. I cannot simply subject you to my categories. I cannot simply see you in terms of my experience. To love you, I must listen to you. I must attend to your voice. I must hear you. If I do not hear you, I cannot love you.

This engagement with women's voices will not simply be across space, but across time. We want to bring ourselves into dialogue with various women in the history of Christianity. We want to draw upon our tradition to be changed by the encounter with the other in our tradition. Our tradition is a living tradition for, as Jaroslav Pelikan has maintained, "Tradition is the living faith of the dead."[24]

Today we will not focus so much on how the structure of androcentrism excluded women and limited women's possibilities for full participation in Western life and in the Christian community; rather, we will attend to women's experiences and recognize their contribution. We will answer the question posed to the foundress of the Sisters of Charity of Leavenworth by her father. Mother Xavier Ross had tried to explain to her father her desire to serve God's people, to which he responded, "What can a woman do?"[25] Well, today we will give a partial answer that question by examining the influence of women throughout Catholic history.

Women as the primary caregivers for children and most probably the principal instructors in their faith had an enormous impact on the world and Church. Women also would have influenced events through the effect they had on their husbands, who would have been active in public life. However, since women were subordinate in an androcentric system, with few exceptions their work and words were not recorded and preserved. The central task of today is to attend to some of those exceptions, to look historically at what women said and did through Catholic Christianity, and to see the impact they had in the public sphere. This is an ongoing task among historians, and we would like to share with you some of the fruits of recent scholarship.

As I have argued, we are by nature ordered to each other and to God as our end. This ordered relation to others is not only across space, but also across time. Those of the past make us who we are today. It is only in engaging in history that I can know myself and know the other. As Archbishop of Canterbury Rowan Williams has said so well,

We recognize ourselves and our concerns in a "distant mirror"… and so are reminded that we are not our own authors, that we have not just discovered what it is to be human, let alone what it is to be Christian. And all this has the important consequence that, if we are free to listen to the strange and recognizable "otherness" of the past, this may help us in dealing with what is strange to us now. An attitude of mind that is not capable of engaging in recognition with the past of the Church is also one that is likely to be closed off from what is different or challenging in the present.[26]

Williams's insistence that listening to the past involves recognizing both its strangeness and its familiarity suggests that as we approach the past, we must avoid two temptations. One temptation is to see a particular period in history as utterly alien to us. It is the temptation to see different periods in the past as so different from our culture and life that they cannot speak to us. The other temptation, which I suggest is much more common, is the temptation not to see particular periods in the past as other or different and to make all sorts of judgments about them without recognizing that it was a different time and a different context. It is the tendency to level out all differences and read one's concerns into the past.

This is particularly true of our topic today and of all other systemic injustices. For instance, we now recognize more clearly than our ancestors the repressive nature of androcentrism as it informed Western culture. In light of this awareness, when we look back at the lives of others who lived in this system, it is tempting to read their experience as the experience of being repressed and shackled by the system. This might be true in some cases; but in other cases, that particular person might not have felt that he or she was repressed at all.

Many women in these contexts were as unaware of androcentrism as Thomas Aquinas was. In many cases, women would identify civil or ecclesiastical authorities as hindering their ability to serve God and God's people but never identified their gender as limiting their possible ways of being and acting in the world. Gender very well might have been the overarching reason, but many did not see it that way, so they did not experience themselves as repressed by the androcentric structures under which they lived.

I make this point simply to stress that we have to be careful not to project our experience onto the experiences of those we will treat today. This point is not intended to brush aside the serious destructiveness of androcentrism I emphasized in the first part of this paper; rather, the hope is that we do not diminish the people we discuss with misplaced pity for them.

Today we will see some of the great figures of Catholic Christianity in a new light: Mary the Mother of God, Mary Magdalene, Teresa of Avila, Thérèse of Lisieux, and Dorothy Day. Less well-known figures will be introduced to many of us for the first time: Phoebe, Junia, Prisca, Thecla, Perpetua, Proba, Egeria, Melania the Elder, Olympias, the Abbess of Las Huelgas in Spain, Brigid of Kildare, Mathilda of Quedlinburg, Isabella of Castile, Mary Ward of England, Leonor Mascarenhas and her daughter Leonor de Vega Osorio, Anne-Marie Javouhey, Mother Theodore Guerin, Cornelia Connelly, and Madeleine Delbrêl. We will in some way make the familiar strange and make the strange familiar.

This is hardly an exhaustive treatment of women who have shaped Catholicism. It is a selection. It is a selection that reflects where we are today for, as you might notice, there are as many laywomen on this list as vowed religious women. This is not to diminish the importance and significance of the vowed religious, but this selection of women serves the purpose of expanding our imagination as to the possibilities of serving within the Catholic Christian community beyond vowed religious life. It serves both to inspire and invigorate the vowed religious and laywomen by showing that even when operating under restrictions, women have had a great impact on the life of the Church.

In his classic nineteenth-century work, *The Civilization of the Renaissance in Italy*, Jacob Burkhardt treats the question, why did the Renaissance begin in Italy? One of the central reasons he gives is the landscape of Italy. People were surrounded by the ruins of antiquity: "ruins of mighty arches and colonnades, half hid in plane-trees, laurels, cypresses and brushwood...."[27] Our intellectual landscape is being altered by the contemporary scholarly excavations and historical reconstructions of women's experiences. Perhaps this new intellectual landscape will lead to a renewal of our Church that, like the renaissance of the fourteenth to seventeenth centuries, will usher in a new humanism that explores, promotes, and defends the full humanity of women. Perhaps it will also call us to a more perfect union that resembles as far as possible the union between the divine persons in the inner life of God.

NOTES

1. John L. Allen Jr., "Lay Ecclesial Ministry and the Feminization of the Church," *National Catholic Reporter*, Vol. 6, No. 43 (June 29, 2007).

2. Most recently, one thinks of women religious of the nineteenth and early-twentieth centuries overseeing large hospitals and health care networks before society gave them the right to vote or before women held comparable jobs to men. This was also true of women religious from the Middle Ages through the nineteenth century, as women would run convents and become abbesses whose powers extended beyond the boundaries of their monastery (see Gary Macy's paper in this collection). This was also true to a certain extent in the early Church, where women in the fourth and fifth centuries founded and directed monasteries. Notice, however, that these opportunities were possible only for celibate women. In reference to the patristic period, Elizabeth Clark writes, "An irony of early Christian history is that the ascetic movement, which had so many features denigrating of women and marriage, became the movement that, more than any other, provided 'liberation' of a sort for Christian women. If they could surmount their identification with sexual and reproductive functioning, women were allowed freedoms and roles they otherwise would not have been granted. I do not posit that most women consciously chose the ascetic life as an 'escape' from marriage. Nonetheless, their renunciations, motivated by religious concerns, served to liberate them from the traditional bonds of marriage. The advantages they received in adopting asceticism were practical as well as theoretical." From "Devil's Gateway and Bride of Christ: Women in the Early Christian World," in Elizabeth A. Clark, *Ascetic Piety and Women's Faith: Essays on Late Ancient Christianity, Studies in Women and Religion*, vol. 20 (Lewiston: Edwin Mellen Press, 1986), p. 42.

3. Elizabeth Clark, *Women in the Early Church, Message of the Fathers of the Church,* vol. 13 (Wilmington, Delaware: Michael Glazier, Inc., 1983), p. 16.

4. For a short account of Galen's and Aretaeus of Cappadocia's views, see Peter Brown, *The Body and Society: Men, Women, and Sexual Renunciation in Early Christianity* (New York: Columbia University Press, 1988), pp. 9-12.

5. Aristotle, *On the Generation of Animals,* 766-768.

6. Ibid., 767a.

7. Gary Wills, *Papal Sin: Structures of Deceit,* (New York: Doubleday, 2000), p. 109. Wills is quoting Clement, *The Educator (Paedagogus)* 2.33 (PG 8.430). I have used Wills's translation of the Greek.

8. Tertullian, *On the Dress of Women,* 1.1 (CSEL 70.59); cited in Elizabeth Clark, *Women in the Early Church,* p. 39.

9. Jerome, Epistle 127 4, 7 (CSEL 56.146); cited in Elizabeth Clark, *Women in the Early Church,* pp. 206-208.

10. Jerome, *Commentary on the Epistle to the Ephesians,* III (5:28) (PL 23, 533); cited in Elizabeth A. Clark "Devil's Gateway and Bride of Christ: Women in the Early Christian World," p. 43.

11. *Summa Theologiae* I q. 92 a. 1 ad. 1. My translation.

12. Center for American Women and Politics, "Women in Elective Office 2008," www.cawp.rutgers. edu (accessed May 20, 2008).

13. *The Beijing Declaration and the Platform for Action* (New York: United Nations, 1996), 2. Cited in Elizabeth A Johnson, *Truly Our Sister: A Theology of Mary in the Communion of Saints* (New York: Continuum, 2003), pp. 19-20.

14. John L. Allen Jr., "Lay Ecclesial Ministry and the Feminization of the Church."

15. Ibid.

16. See U.S. Conference of Catholic Bishops, "Consultation with Women in Diocesan Leadership: A Report by the Bishops Committee on Women in Society and in the Church" (Washington, DC: USCCB, 2001) at www.usccb.org/laity/women/report.shtml.

17. John XXIII, *Pacem in Terris,* § 41.

18. John H. Wright, S.J. "A Theological Analysis of Freedom in Terms of Grace," in *Proceedings of the Catholic College Teachers of Sacred Doctrine, 11th Annual Convention,* 1965, p. 83.

19. Ibid., p. 83.

20. Ibid., p. 84.

21. Ibid., p. 84.

22. John H. Wright, S.J., "The Eternal Plan of Divine Providence," *Theological Studies* 27, no. 1 (1966), p. 38.

23. Murdoch, "The Sublime and the Good," in *Existentials and Mystics: Writings on Philosophy and Literature,* ed. Peter Conradi (New York: Penguin Books, 1999), p. 215.

24. Jaroslav Pelikan, *The Vindication of Tradition,* (New Haven: Yale University Press), p. 65.

25 Sisters of Charity of Leavenworth website, "Who are We," www.scls.org/Who_Are_We/who_history.html (accessed on May 16, 2008).

26 Rowan Williams, *Why Study the Past: The Quest for the Historical Church* (Grand Rapids, Michigan: Wm. B. Eerdmans, 2005), p. 111.

27. Jacob Burkhardt, *The Civilization of the Renaissance in Italy: An Essay,* 2nd ed., (Oxford: Phaidon Press, 1981), pp. 113-114.

2. Women in the New Testament

Susan A. Calef, PhD, Assistant Professor of Theology and Director of Graduate Studies in Theology
Creighton University

In his introduction to the book *Pioneer Women: Voices From the Kansas Frontier*, historian Arthur Schlesinger, Jr., remarked, "Women have constituted the most spectacular casualty of history."[28] Indeed, mention of America's western frontier, for example, conjures up the figures of Wild Bill Hickok and Buffalo Bill, Jesse James and General Custer, cowboys and Indians, gunslingers and lawmen. Women, if visible at all on this mindscape, are reduced to stereotype or myth, for example, the notorious Calamity Jane or the madam with a heart of gold exemplified by Miss Kitty of *Gunsmoke* fame. Similarly, a litany of men's names dominates early Christian history: Peter and Paul, James, John and, slightly later, Ignatius and Irenaeus, Justin and Polycarp.

Thankfully, the absence of women from History with a capital H, by which I mean the recorded past, and worse yet, the absence of women and their accomplishments from our consciousness, are being rectified thanks in large part to the impact of the women's movement and emergence of feminism.[29] The two waves of the women's movement wrought enormous changes on the cultural landscape, and so, too, in the Academy. In the wake of the second wave in the 1960s, women have entered the Academy in significant numbers, with the result that scholarship in any field, including theology and biblical studies, is no longer a males-only affair. In our work as scholars and educators, we women (and some of our male colleagues) are asking new questions, including in this case, where are the bodies, the faces, the voices of women who traversed these terrains—early Christian, and centuries later, the American—as surely as did the men?

It is now widely acknowledged that traditional historiography has been *partial* in both senses of the word; that is, *partial* to the perspectives, words, and deeds of the relatively few elite men of power, and *partial* as in only part of the whole story. As a result, women and non-elite men were, in effect, consigned to the "dustbin" of history. Modern social historians, determined to construct a more complete picture of our past, therefore devised techniques with which to achieve "the silent, mathematical resurrection of a total past."[30]

By means of that "resurrection," women are being raised up, restored to, and taking their rightful place in the historical record and so, too, on our mindscapes. It is my joy and privilege as a New Testament scholar to witness this "resurrection" of the women that is currently occurring and to bring the Good News of it to you here today. This "rising" of the women who have gone before us, in this case our foremothers and sisters in faith, is a work of more than scholarly consequence, for it restores to women our story, a story that can enlighten and empower, and provides for both genders a richer, more complete story by which to imagine our future.

Reflective of recent currents in culture and Academy, this conference turns our attention to the women who have been part of, who have served, and who have contributed to the Church from its inception. It is my task to take us back to the beginning, to the New Testament period and the women whose presence and activities may be glimpsed in the Gospels and the letters of Paul. I will focus our attention on women of two generations to which New Testament texts afford access: the originating generation—Jesus and those around him in his reign of God movement; and the first generation—Paul and his contemporaries, who participated in the ongoing mission that originated with the Jesus movement.

With respect to the originating generation, Part I will address the question most frequently posed by audiences today: what role did women play in Jesus' movement? Pursuit of that question will lead us in Part II to the figure of Mary Magdalene, who now enjoys celebrity status of sorts, thanks to Dan Brown's *The Da Vinci Code*. Finally, Part III turns our attention to the women in the earliest postresurrection communities glimpsed in the New Testament, the communities addressed by Paul in his letters. His correspondence with those communities provides tantalizing, indeed precious, glimpses of women at work in the mission, including the three about whom we know somewhat more than most: Phoebe, Prisca, and Junia.

Be advised, however, that revising the historical record is fraught with difficulty due to the scarcity and nature of the sources.[31] In the case of the New Testament period to which we now turn, we may recover something of women's activities but, regrettably, women's own voices are nowhere to be heard in Pauline and Gospel texts. Therefore, we cannot recover the subjective experience of the women we seek to know.[32] Their dreams, desires, and discontents, their schemes, strivings, and strategies are, unfortunately, lost to us.

Part I. The Originating Generation:
Women of the Jesus Movement

In the modern era, numerous scholars have devoted enormous energy to what is known as the quest for the historical Jesus. Informed by the methods and conclusions of that quest, others have undertaken a comparable project, what I term the quest for the historical women of the Jesus movement. These two related quests must rely primarily on a single source of information: the four canonical Gospels. Surprisingly, women appear more often in the pages of the Gospels than one might expect, given the patriarchal and androcentric culture in which they were written. Jesus' outreach in ministry to those in need clearly included many women and girls. One thinks, for example, of the hemorrhaging woman (see Mark 5:24b–34), the woman bent double (see Luke 13:10–17), Jairus' daughter (see Mark 5:22–24,35–43), the widow of Nain whose son had died (see Luke 7:11–17), the adulterous woman about to be stoned (see John 8:2–11), and my personal favorite, the feisty Syro-Phoenician woman (see Mark 7:24–30) who, in a remarkable exchange, dared to talk back to authority, the only character in all the Gospels to prod Jesus into a change of mind.

As engaging as the stories of Jesus' encounters with these women are, they will not be our focus here. Their stories, however, make one wonder whether women were simply passive recipients of his ministry, fortunate objects of his merciful outreach, or active participants in his reign-of-God movement. If they did join and participate in the movement, what was their status in it?

We commonly think of those around Jesus in terms of a number of groups whose designations are drawn from the Gospels—for example, disciples, apostles, the Twelve, the crowds, the multitudes. Our question, then: Where did women fit among them? Did women belong to the inner circles around Jesus? Answering this question is not easy for various reasons, some of them having to do with the varied and somewhat confusing ways in which the evangelists use the terms *the Twelve*," "disciples," and "apostles," and others having to do with our own tendencies as Christian interpreters. Often we assume we know who belongs to these groups, but our assumptions reflect neither the usage characteristic of a particular Gospel nor the historical reality that may or may not be faithfully reflected in the evangelists' use of the terms.[33] Today most Christians, for example, refer to the innermost circle around Jesus as the Twelve Apostles and assume that the term *apostle* is synonymous with *the Twelve;* thus, the Twelve were apostles, and the apostles were twelve and only twelve.

Historical research, however, belies this popular assumption.[34] For, in fact, a careful examination of the Gospels reveals that the term *apostle*, from the Greek *apostolos*) is relatively infrequent in the Gospels, particularly in comparison to occurrences of *disciple* (Greek, *mathētēs*) and that the term *apostle* is not restricted to twelve men.[35] Mark, the earliest canonical Gospel, and John, the latest, never use the phrases *the Twelve Disciples* or *the Twelve Apostles*. Rather, they use *the Twelve* absolutely (Mark 6:7; John 6:67), without further qualification or specification.[36] The earliest Gospel, Mark, uses the word *apostolos* only once in his Gospel (6:30), where it refers to the Twelve when they return from a temporary mission; after that, the term disappears from the narrative. Thus, *apostles* indicates a temporary function that the Twelve sometimes discharge.[37] This Markan usage suggests that during Jesus' public ministry, *apostle* (Aramaic, *šĕlîâh*; Greek, *apostolos*) was probably not used by him or his disciples as a fixed term for a particular group of his followers. At most, an Aramaic word like *šĕlîhîn* ("messengers," "envoys") may have been used in an *ad hoc* sense when Jesus sent the Twelve out on a temporary mission (Mark 6:30; Matthew 10:2).[38] Therefore, because use of the word *apostle* can be misleading when thinking about the groups with which Jesus interacted, we would do well to follow the lead of Mark and John and use *the Twelve*, not *the apostles*, for the innermost circle of twelve men.[39]

Two further conclusions of historical-Jesus research are pertinent for our interest. First, it is clear, based on the multiple criteria used to identify authentic Jesus traditions, that Jesus gathered around himself a group of committed disciples that was larger than twelve; and second, *disciples* were those called by Jesus to a literal, physical following on his preaching tours around Palestine, an accompaniment requiring that they leave behind the comforts of home, family, and occupation and accept the hardships partici-pation in his reign-of-God movement would entail. Our question, then: Do the Gospels provide evidence that some women met those requirements, that some women were called by Jesus to leave home and family to join his itinerant reign-of-God movement?

The evidence by which to draw our conclusions is not clear-cut and un-equivocal. On the one hand, Mark 15:40–41 (see parallel passages in Matthew 27:55–56 and Luke 23:49) informs us that at the cross.

There were also women looking on from a distance; among them were Mary Magdalene, and Mary the mother of James the younger and of Joses, and Salome. These used to follow him and provided for him when he was in Galilee; and there were many other women who had come up with him to Jerusalem.

These verses evidence that women did indeed travel with Jesus and that they accompanied him to Jerusalem at Passover.[40] The likelihood that women were a part of Jesus' peripatetic entourage is supported by Luke 8:1–3, which depicts a group of women traveling with Jesus and the Twelve from place to place.[41] Therefore, we have reason to conclude that a group of devoted women followers did accompany Jesus around Galilee and finally up to Jerusalem. The presence of the women at the crucifixion of Jesus in Mark 15:40–41 and synoptic parallels appears to be historically accurate because it is independently confirmed by John 19:25.

This Gospel evidence that women followed Jesus in a literal, physical sense suggests they were disciples. There is, however, a problem that cannot be ignored: Although the Gospels frequently refer to "disciples" (Greek singular, *mathētēs*; Greek plural, *mathētai*), often without further specifying their identities, the word *disciple* is never applied to any of the women or to the group of women followers when they are mentioned apart from men followers.[42] Why that is might have something to do with another noteworthy feature of the Gospels: They contain stories of the calls of men, for example, Simon Peter, Andrew, the sons of Zebedee (Mark 1:16–20), and Levi (Mark 2:14), but nothing comparable for any woman, including the women followers whose names we know. Does this perhaps suggest that those women—Mary Magdalene, Joanna, Salome—were not disciples?

Several plausible explanations exist for this glaring absence in Gospel testimony. The evangelists might have known of such stories but chose not to include them for some reason about which we can only speculate.[43] On the other hand, perhaps due to the vagaries of oral tradition within a patriarchal and androcentric context, the evangelists simply did not know of any stories of Jesus calling women, which does not mean that such a call did not happen. Alternatively, perhaps the "call" of women happened differently due to the cultural constraints on the interactions between women and men. Given what we know of prevailing gender codes, for example, it is debatable whether Jesus would have or could have enlisted women to the cause in the same way he called specific men.[44] Those same gender codes, however, also make it somewhat implausible that Palestinian-Jewish women could have hit the road with Jesus and a band of men without some kind of recruitment or assent by Jesus.[45]

In any case, the lack of call stories in the tradition would likely incline the evangelists not to apply the title *disciple* to his women followers. In addition, and perhaps most importantly, that the evangelists do not designate any women *disciples* may be explained linguistically. At the time of Jesus, the words *disciple* and *disciples* existed in Hebrew and Aramaic only in masculine forms: *talmîd* and *talmîdîm* in Hebrew, *talmîdā'* and *talmîdayyā'* in Aramaic.[46] Thus, it might be that during his public ministry Jesus had committed women followers whom he conceived of as full participants in his movement, but there was no feminine noun that said "female disciple" by which to describe them. The evangelists, therefore, had no basis for designating the women *disciples* in writing their Gospels.[47]

In any case, the lack of call stories and the absence of the designation *disciple* in reference to women ought not obscure the reality to which Gospel tradition attests. Some women embarked on a literal, physical following of Jesus, by which presumably they had access to Jesus' teaching. In doing so, apparently, like their male counterparts, they were willing to endure whatever hardships and hostility participation in his movement entailed, including the misunderstanding of their fellow villagers, in whose eyes their conduct—traveling with a band of men—was likely scandalous, perhaps even sinful.[48] We have no evidence they were called in the same way some men were called, so how and why these women became part of the movement is unclear. Perhaps their experience of Jesus' powerful healing prompted—indeed, compelled—them to join the movement. Even in the absence of a verbal call comparable to those addressed to the Twelve and to other men disciples, however, there is reason to surmise that these women were not less-valued members of the movement. The women, like the men, were a compelling sign of Jesus' mission on behalf of the reign of God: the Twelve as symbol of the end-time regathering of the tribes of Israel, the healed women as living proof of the eschatological liberation that commences with the coming reign of God. And so, in answer to our question, did the Historical Jesus have women disciples? I am persuaded by the conclusion, "In name, no; in reality—putting aside the question of an implicit as opposed to an explicit call—yes."[49]

The synoptic references to women traveling with Jesus compel still another question. If women accompanied Jesus to Jerusalem for Passover, as the synoptic references suggest, were women present at the Last Supper? Or to state it a bit more playfully, who cooked the Last Supper?[50] This question, despite its playful formulation, serves the serious purpose of exposing the comparative invisibility of women in the Gospels, in traditional biblical interpretation, in much preaching, and so too in our religious imaginations. For when reference is made to the Last Supper, what image comes to mind? Most Christians, I suspect, imagine something quite like Leonardo da Vinci's *Last Supper*, the classic rendering of Jesus' last meal painted almost 1500 years after the event. This painting, like those by Raphael, Rosselli, Dali, among many others, depicts Jesus surrounded by twelve men in a private room.

But have you ever asked whether this visual representation of the Last Supper as a "men only" affair is historically accurate?[51] The results of recent scholarship provide reason to do so. Indeed, in light of the results of Historical Jesus research and of recent study of dining practices in the Hellenistic world, questions are being raised that advise against any claim to certainty about the historical reality, and so, permit some re-imaging.[52] Recall that both Mark and Luke indicate that women accompanied Jesus in his travels, including to Jerusalem, and that in doing so, they engaged in *diēkonoun*. Significantly, the Greek verb *diakoneō*, means "to wait on at table" or "to serve," suggests the presence of women at meals with Jesus, at the very least in a food-service capacity.[53] If these women prepared and shared meals with Jesus and his band when they were on the road, are we to think they would not continue to do so when he is in Jerusalem? Regardless of whether the Last Supper was a Passover meal, as the synoptic Gospels attest, or simply a last fellowship meal, as John depicts, we have reason to question whether Jesus' last meal was really the kind of exclusive table fellowship we have come to imagine.

The Gospels, after all, attest that Jesus practiced an inclusive table fellow-ship that disturbed some parties (Mark 2:17; Luke 15:1–2).[54] Is it likely that in Jerusalem Jesus suddenly would depart from the inclusive practice that had characterized his movement? The synoptic Gospels, on the other hand, depict the Last Supper as the Passover meal. If this festal meal was a family ritual, as is generally thought, is it likely that Jesus would eat the meal only with twelve men? Given Jesus' radical redefinition of family, "Whoever does the will of God is my brother and sister and mother" (Mark 3:35), one must ask, where are the "sisters and mothers"?[55] Are we to imagine that the women who engaged in *diēkonoun* on the journey to Jerusalem would not continue this activity upon arrival in the city? And if their *diēkonoun* continued, are we to imagine that after preparing the Passover meal they departed or were dismissed? Where would they go, and with whom would these unattached women eat the festal meal? Indeed, who cooked—and ate—the Last Supper? This deliberately provocative question deserves further investigation for, as one commentator has observed, "That Jesus excluded most of his disciples, including women, from his last meal, whether or not this was a Passover meal, contradicts both the Judaism which nurtured him and also the table-praxis of his ministry."[56]

Some object that men and women did not eat together in the ancient world and that segregation of the sexes at mealtime was standard Jewish practice as well. Research into meals and dining practices in the Hellenistic period, however, indicates that dining conventions were changing, including among Jews. We now have evidence for participation of Jewish women in meals with men, even in Palestine.[57] Indeed, Gospel traditions indicate that Jesus dined in the presence of men and women. Both Luke and John, for example, include stories of Jesus dining with Mary and Martha (Luke 10:38–42; John 12:1–8). Elsewhere, women come to Jesus when he is dining, and there is no indication that he is uncomfortable about this or that the other men at the table object to their presence as improper (see parallel passages in Mark 14:3–9, Matthew 26:6–13; Luke 7:36–50; John 12:1–8).[58] Scenes such as these, together with evidence for women's *diēkonoun* (Mark 15:40–41) and the charge that Jesus ate with tax collectors and sinners suggest men and women could be together at meals, moreover, that Jesus did indeed dine with women. If that is the case, why should we think it would be any different at Passover in Jerusalem, especially when women followers accompanied him there and had engaged regularly in *diēkonoun*?[59]

If one is persuaded of the plausibility, even likelihood, that Jesus' last meal was shared with more than the Twelve, how do we account for the Gospel depiction of the Last Supper as an exclusively male affair of Jesus and the Twelve? Kathleen Corley's study of meals in the Gospel tradition concludes, "These early traditions linking women disciples to Jesus' meals strongly suggests that the 'Last Supper' traditions which limit his intimate circle to men are *later* [emphasis mine] literary creations which cast Jesus' meals with his disciples as all-male symposia, or 'drinking parties,' in accordance with stereotypical Greco-Roman literary conventions."[60] Fortunately, careful study permits us to glimpse the historical reality that stands behind the literary representations: the radical Jewish prophet and sage who was apparently unconstrained by conventional dining practice, including symposium etiquette.[61]

Part II. Mary Magdalene, Apostle to the Apostles (*Apostolorum Apostola*)

Let us turn now to a quest for the Historical Mary Magdalene, who was evidently one of the women who accompanied Jesus and engaged in *diēkonoun*. Unfortunately, our quest for this woman is hampered by the scarcity of information. The earliest and most reliable are the four canonical Gospels; and yet, because the Gospels are narrative proclamations of the Good News of and about Jesus, they are only incidentally about Mary Magdalene or any of the male disciples, for that matter. It is not a surprise, then, that they contain only twelve references to her, eleven of which are confined to the story of Jesus' passion, death, and resurrection.[62] This means we can know far less than we might wish about her role during his ministry. Nevertheless, from these incidental references emerges the following impressionistic sketch.

The four Gospels refer to her not as Mary Magdalene, our customary designation, but as Mary the Magdalene, or in Luke, Mary who "was called the Magdalene" (8:2). The surname *the Magdalene*, which is assumed to derive from her place of origin, Magdala, distinguishes her from the other Marys who are frequent companions in Gospel scenes. The location of Magdala between Nazareth, Jesus' hometown, and Capernaum, his apparent base of operations during his reign-of-God movement, might suggest Mary was among his first followers, having encountered him even before the movement was based in Capernaum. Magdala was a fishing town on the Sea of Galilee and so, if she had any connection to the fishing business, perhaps she met Jesus along the shore, as had Simon Peter, Andrew, and the sons of Zebedee. That she is identified solely by place of origin and not by relationship to a man, as other women are (for example, Mary the wife of Clopas, Mary the mother of Joses), indicates that she was an independent woman. Unfortunately, we know nothing of the circumstances that led to what would have been for a woman in that time and culture an unconventional status—independent of a husband, father, or son.

That status perhaps had something to do with what Luke tells us about her in the only reference to Mary Magdalene outside of the passion and resurrection narratives. According to Luke 8:1–3, she and other women "who had been cured of evil spirits and infirmities" along with the Twelve accompanied Jesus from village to village, providing for him out of their resources. Mary Magdalene is further described as one "from whom seven demons had gone out" (8:2; also Mark 16:9). We do not know precisely what that says about her.[63] There is no evidence that this suggests the kind of sexual promiscuity that would earn her the brand "whore," but possession by demons would likely account for her evident lack of marital and familial ties, as Tobit 3:7–17 confirms.[64] In addition, it is not difficult to imagine that if Jesus was the one who freed her from this affliction, which is not explicitly stated in the text but would cohere with his exorcistic activity, she might well desire to throw in her lot with him and his movement, as apparently she did, even to his death and burial.

It is, above all, Mary Magdalene's presence at cross and tomb that the Gospel tradition has preserved for us. Hers is the first among the names of a group of women who, after following Jesus and providing for him in Galilee, went up with him to Jerusalem, where they witnessed his brutal crucifixion and death (Mark 15:40–41; Matthew 27:56). John alone places her at the foot of the cross with his mother, the beloved disciple, and other blood kin (John 19:25). Both Mark and Matthew report that after the crucifixion she went with one or more other women to visit the grave (Mark 15:47; Matthew 27:61; 28:1), returning after the Sabbath was over to anoint him (Mark 16:1; Luke 24:1). That she is consistently named first in these scenes suggests her prominence among Jesus' women followers. While at the tomb, she and the other women were the first to experience a vision in which a heavenly messenger announces the Good News of Jesus' resurrection (Mark 16:1–8; Matthew 28:1–10; Luke 24:1–11). Finally, and most important, according to John 20:1–18, Mary Magdalene was the first recipient of a resurrection appearance as well as the first to be sent to the disciples with a message from the Risen Christ. It is this tradition in John that earned her the designation *Apostolorum Apostola*, apostle to the apostles, a title repeated as late as Thomas Aquinas in the Middle Ages.[65]

Unfortunately, Mary Magdalene's status as "apostle to the apostles" has, for centuries, been effaced by the image that dominates the imagination of Catholic and Protestant alike, that of a penitent prostitute saved from her sinful ways by Jesus.[66] Scholars agree, however, that there is no evidence in early Christian sources that Mary Magdalene was a prostitute. This raises the question of how and why this popular misconception came to dominate the Christian imagination. The explanation proffered by Dan Brown's characters, that it "is the legacy of a smear campaign...by the early Church" concocted to cover up her true role as "the Holy Grail" does not bear up under scrutiny. A sermon of Pope Gregory the Great appears to have had a role in firmly establishing the misconception in the tradition;[67] but there is no evidence that Gregory or any other Churchmen deliberately branded her with, in effect, the scarlet letter of prostitution in a malicious act of ecclesiastical foul play.

The explanation is far less sinister, though no less regrettable: a confusion of Mary Magdalene with two unnamed women in the Gospels—the sinful woman of Luke 7:36–50 and the adulterous woman of John 8:3–11—and with the Mary who anointed Jesus in John 12:3–8. The Catholic Church rectified this erroneous interpretation in its 1970 revision of the *Roman Missal*, removing the designation *penitent* from its description of her and changing the Gospel reading for her feast from the story of the sinful woman to that of her vision of the Risen Lord at the tomb (John 20:1–18). Unfortunately, the Church's official correction of this case of mistaken identity has gone largely unnoticed, much like an obscure footnote no one has bothered to read. It's fortunate that Dan Brown's megabestseller will have accomplished what

Church and Academy have not managed: putting an end to the "harlotization" of Mary Magdalene in the popular imagination. The label "penitent prostitute" has for far too long eclipsed her witness to the resurrection and her role as "apostle to the apostles."[68]

III. Women in the Pauline Mission Field

Fortunately, the Pauline letters afford more direct access to the demographics of early Christian communities, including their women, than do the Gospels. From these letters and Acts of the Apostles, one scholar has compiled a Christian Who's Who of almost eighty persons, of whom approximately one fifth are women.[69] Let us begin with the tantalizing glimpses of women in the Corinthian and Philippian communities before turning to the single most informative source of information about women in the Pauline mission field, Romans 16.

1 Corinthians

Paul writes 1 Corinthians in response to both a letter the community had sent (7:1) and a report about problems in the community delivered by a delegation designated as "Chloe's people" (1:11). Chloe is one of only two women named in the letter (see Prisca 16:19). Who her "people" are is not indicated. Her mention apart from a man suggests that she headed her own household; therefore, her "people" were probably slaves or freed persons of her household. That Paul expects the name to be recognized by the Corinthians suggests Chloe was a figure of prominence in the community; she and her household were perhaps the nucleus of a congregation that met in her house. In any case, this brief mention introduces us, at the very least, to a woman who takes initiative on behalf of the community, seeking the counsel of its founder when divisiveness threatened its membership (1:11–13).

Similarly, 1 Corinthians 11:2–16 provides another window onto the presence and activity of the women of the Corinthian community. Through it we learn that women prayed and prophesied in the Christian assembly (11:5). Prophecy was among the esteemed gifts (*charismata*) given by the Spirit (12:7–11) for the building up of the Church (14:1–12);d apparently the Spirit, unconstrained by society's status- and gender-bound channels of authority, distributed this gift to women as well as men. That women's prayer and prophecy were a regular and accepted occurrence in the community is clearly indicated by the focus of Paul's argument that "any woman who prays or prophesies with her head unveiled disgraces her head" (11:5). Evidently the women prophets are not covering their heads during the assembly, and it is *that* to which Paul strenuously objects. Their right to pray and prophesy in the assembly is not contested; rather, it seems taken for granted.[70]

A bit later in the letter, however, Paul enjoins, "As in all the Churches of the saints, women should be silent in the Churches. For they are not permitted to speak, but should be subordinate, as the law also says. If there is anything they desire to know, let them ask their husbands at home. For it is shameful for a woman to speak in Church" (14:33b–35). It's curious that Paul's injunction, which conforms to the societal expectation that women remain silent when in public space, appears to contradict his stance in 11:5, which assumes women are free to pray and prophesy in the assembly, albeit with heads veiled. Whether there is a contradiction need not concern us here.[71] It is the evidence of women's activities that is noteworthy for our purposes: Some married women were speaking out in the assembly. Further information about their identity and speech emerges from the question Paul poses in an attempt to silence them: "Or did the word of God originate with you?" The phrase "word of God" suggests these women were uttering inspired or ecstatic speech, hence, that they were prophetesses who felt entitled to weigh, even debate, what was said in the assembly.[72] Hence, "Let them ask their husbands at home" is Paul's seemingly exasperated response to what one commentator aptly describes as the "virtual cacophony of individual expressions" that resulted.[73]

Philippians

Paul's letter to the Philippians, supplemented by the Acts of the Apostles, affords us a glimpse of women in another community the apostle had founded. Acts informs us that many women were converted by Paul's Gospel, among them one named Lydia, "a seller of purple, of the city of Thyatira" (Acts 16:13–15, 40). Gathered with other women on the sabbath, Lydia was a "god-fearer" (a gentile worshipper of the Jewish God) who, upon hearing Paul's preaching, converted and was baptized along with her household. In the absence of mention of a husband, we may surmise she was the female head of her household. Luke also tells us she welcomed the apostle and his associates into her home and that subsequently the Church met in her house (16:15, 40). That Lydia owned a home large enough to accommodate guests and host a house-church suggests she was a woman of some means. It is likely her resources were related to her business, as the purple goods in which she dealt were a coveted luxury item sold at a high price in antiquity.[74] If the Lukan account is historically accurate, then the Church at Philippi was founded among women and first met in the home of Lydia, an independent merchant woman with material and spiritual authority over her household.

Elsewhere in the letter Paul names two women, Euodia and Syntyche (4:2), who if the information in Acts 16 about Lydia is accurate, follow in her footsteps in the Philippian Church. Apparently, there is strife between the two, and so Paul writes, "I urge Euodia and I urge Syntyche to be of the same mind in the Lord" (4:2). Unfortunately, nothing in the reference allows us to determine the nature of the strife between them.[75] In any case, his explicit request that an unidentified figure he addresses as "loyal companion" help these women, includes an explanation of why they deserve assistance: "they have struggled beside me in the work of the Gospel together with Clement and the rest of my co-workers" (4:3). The image of struggling side by side as in an athletic contest affirms the equal footing on which these women work with Paul and other male workers and indicates that they, too, are his co-workers. Elsewhere, Paul uses the term *co-worker* (or fellow worker) to refer to itinerant workers who traveled to spread the Gospel; therefore, we may surmise that Euodia and Syntyche were a missionary team dedicated to Gospel proclamation.[76] That the strife between these women is of express concern to Paul suggests their prominence in the community.[77]

Romans

The single most informative yet neglected testimony to the activities of the earliest generation of Christian women is the list of greetings in Romans 16.[78] Among the twenty-seven persons Paul greets by name are ten women: Phoebe, Prisca, Mary, Junia, Tryphaena and Tryphosa, Persis, Julia, the mother of Rufus, and the sister of Nereus. We may suppose that still more women were among "the family of Aristobulus" (16:10), "the family of Narcissus" (16:11), and "all the saints" (16:15). Fortunately, for our purposes, Paul does more than name names. This seemingly innocuous list of greetings includes a variety of terms that illumine the various functional roles members of the community, men and women alike, assumed: deacon or minister, patron, co-worker, and apostle. Now let's determine who's who.

Paul singles out four of the ten women for their work or labor: "Mary, who has worked very hard among you" (16:6); "those workers in the Lord, Tryphaena and Tryphosa" (16:12), and "beloved Persis, who has worked hard in the Lord" (16:12). Elsewhere Paul uses the verb *working* or *laboring (kopiontes)* for various works in the missionary enterprise and the building up of the communities. According to 1 Corinthians 16:15, the co-workers and laborers are those who have "devoted themselves to the service (*diakonia*) of the saints." That the role of laborer was invested with authority is indicated by Paul's admonition to the Corinthians to "put yourselves at the service of such people" (16:16). Similarly, he urged the Thessalonians to "respect those who labor among you, and have charge of you in the Lord and admonish you; esteem them very highly in love because of their work" (1 Thessalonians 5:12).[79] We may suppose, then, that these four women whose work Paul deems worthy of mention shared in the authority of such "laborers."

Paul's references to three other women provide more detailed information about each. At the head of the list of greetings is the equivalent of a letter or note of recommendation not unlike that given for Timothy elsewhere (16:10–11). Paul writes, "I commend to you our sister Phoebe, a deacon of the Church at Cenchreae, so that you may welcome her in the Lord as is fitting for the saints, and help her in whatever she may require from you, for she has been a benefactor of many and of myself as well" (16:1–2). Her mythological name suggests Phoebe was a Gentile, perhaps a freedwoman. In the absence of mention of a husband, she, like Lydia, appears to have been independent of a patriarchal household. Paul introduces Phoebe to the Roman Christians in hopes they will extend proper hospitality to her. His commendation also probably implies that Phoebe had been authorized to carry his letter to the Roman community. Thus, we glimpse a woman serving the Church in an itinerant capacity.

Phoebe is recommended to the hospitality of Christians in terms of two substantive titles—"*diakonos* of the Church at Cenchreae" and "*prostatis* of many and myself as well." Unfortunately, English translations of the text have tended to obscure the significance of these designations. For example, when *diakonos* is used in reference to Paul or another man, commentators translate it to "minister," "servant," "missionary," or "deacon." In the case of Phoebe, however, *diakonos* is most often rendered as the rather generic "servant" (e.g., in the King James Version [KJV], New American Standard Bible [NASB], New International Version [NIV]) or "deaconess" (in the Amplified Bible [AB]), the latter construed in terms of the later deaconess (*diakonissa*) whose position within the hierarchy of roles that eventually emerged was clearly subordinate and whose duties were gender-specific: caring for the sick and poor of her own gender, instructing women catechumens, being present at interviews of women with bishops, priests, or deacons, and assisting at the baptism of women.[80]

Phoebe, however, is termed *diakonos*, the masculine form of the noun, not the feminine *diakonissa*. Although it is not exactly clear what a *diakonos* did in this early period, we have no indication that it involved gender-specific responsibilities and therefore that Phoebe's work was restricted solely to women. Unless there is evidence to the contrary, we should assume that at this early stage of the Christian movement the functions of male and female *diakonoi* were similar.

Indeed, Pauline usage ought to be the determining factor in translation and interpretation of such terms. Analysis of the terminology Paul uses for his circle of associates reveals frequent use of the term *diakonos* in tandem with *co-worker* (*synergos*) and *worker* (*ergates*), both of which refer to itinerant workers. More precisely, the term is used with reference to preaching activity and also with those entrusted to teach the mysteries of God; thus, *diakonos* designates a special class of co-workers engaged in preaching or teaching, as missionaries, or as workers in local congregations.[81] In Phoebe's case, the occurrence of the possessive qualifier "of the Church of Cenchreae" suggests she is a local leader, one who nevertheless travels, whether on her own business or as an official representative of the community. Galatians 6:6 implies that this type of worker deserved to be remunerated by the community; therefore, since nothing in Paul's letters indicates that only men were "real *diakonoi*," we may imagine that the *diakonos* Phoebe was paid for her service. Indeed, the use of *diakonoi* in Philippians 1:1, where it appears in tandem with *episkopoi*, confirms that *diakonos* was some kind of recognized function or emerging office within the community. Therefore, for this instance of *diakonos*, the translation "minister" (NAB) or "deacon" (New Revised Standard Version [NRSV]) is preferable to "servant."[82]

The second title that the minister Phoebe bears, prostatis, has been trans-lated "helper" or "of great help" (in NASB , AB, NIV), "succourer of many" (KJV), and "hath assisted" (Douay-Rheims). Again, this translation has the effect of obscuring the significance of her activity and assigning her a subor-dinate role. In contemporaneous literature, the term often meant "leading of-ficer," "president," or "superintendent." In this instance, however, it is difficult to see how this meaning could be intended, because Paul claims Phoebe was a *prostatis* of many and of himself. Another of its attested meanings seems far more likely, that is, *prostatis*, which is equivalent to the Latin patrona, meaning "patron" or "benefactor" (NAB, NRSV). The title suggests Phoebe had some wealth at her disposal and acted as a patron of many Christians, including Paul. This is plausible, given what we know of women's patronage of groups in the Greco-Roman world.[83] Both private associations and Christian groups depended in part on the beneficence of wealthier persons, including women, whose patronage consisted of financial support and hospitality as well as exertion of influence and connections on behalf of clients. Apparently

Paul and many others stood in a patron-client relationship with Phoebe; so, in accordance with the exchange law of Greco-Roman patronage, he requests that the Roman community give her whatever she needs during her stay as repayment for her benefactions Paul and others, as clients, owed her.

A further intriguing suggestion regarding Phoebe is worth noting. A recent commentator contends that in her capacity as patron, Phoebe had agreed to underwrite the mission to Spain, a project of vital significance to Paul and to the letter he is writing (Romans 15:24–5). The text of Romans 16 was written, then, in anticipation of her departure for Rome, where she was to create the logistical base for the Spanish mission while Paul was delivering the Jerusalem collection. According to this theory, what Paul was requesting for Phoebe was not simply the hospitality due a patron, but cooperation with her in the patronage this mission would require. The list of greetings that follows Phoebe's commendation is comparable, then, to "a roster of potential campaign supporters that political operatives bring into a city as they begin to establish a campaign for their candidate."[84] If this hypothesis is correct, Phoebe bore authority to do far more than deliver the mail.

Paul's commendation of Phoebe is followed by his greeting to Prisca (or the diminutive form, Priscilla, in Acts), one of the few women mentioned more than once in the New Testament. Not only Paul (Romans 16:3; 1 Corinthians 16:19) but Luke (Acts 18: 2–3, 18, 26–27) and one of the Pastorals (2 Tim 4:19) preserve memory of her, always with Aquila, who is presumed to have been her husband. The remarkable fact that Prisca's name is mentioned before her husband's in four of these occurrences (Romans 16:3; 2 Timothy 4:19; Acts 18:18, 26) is generally interpreted as suggesting either her higher social status or her greater prominence in the Christian community.

The couple appears in Acts 18 in the context of Paul's second missionary journey. There Luke tells us that in Corinth, Paul encountered "a Jew named Aquila, a native of Pontus, who had recently come from Italy with his wife Priscilla, because Claudius had ordered all Jews to leave Rome. Paul went to see them, and, because he was of the same trade, he stayed with them, and they worked together—by trade they were tentmakers" (Acts 18:2–3). From this we learn, first, that Priscilla and her husband were Jews and that they were Christians before meeting Paul. When Claudius banished Jews from Rome, they moved to Corinth, where they accepted Paul as a co-worker in their trade of leatherworking or tent-making. Apparently by the time Paul arrived, they were well established in the city and had a house into which they welcomed Paul, providing him with shelter and work.

The Lukan account further informs us about this couple in 18:24–26. After accompanying Paul to Ephesus where he took leave of them, Priscilla and Aquila encountered Apollos, an eloquent Jewish Christian from Alexandria, who spoke boldly in the synagogue (18:24–26), but apparently not accurately enough. "When Priscilla and Aquila heard him," Luke tells us, "they took him aside and explained the way of God to him more accurately" (18:26). Evidently their instruction of Apollos was effective, for two verses later Luke reports a success for which the couple would seem to deserve partial credit: in Achaia "he [Apollos] powerfully confuted the Jews in public, showing by the Scriptures that the Christ was Jesus" (18:28). Thus, we meet here an early Christian woman knowledgeable enough to correct the insufficient teachings of the learned Alexandrian.[85]

Paul's greeting of the couple in Romans 6:3–4 enables us to elaborate the picture sketched in Acts 18:1–28. There Paul speaks of Prisca, together with Aquila, as "my fellow workers (*synergous*) in Christ Jesus," indicating that she and her husband were itinerant missionaries. Their work as tentmakers likely underwrote the couple's missionary activities, while their missionary travels provided new venues in which to ply their trade. New Testament references that allow us to trace some of their movements attest the role of travel in their lives as missionary artisans: from Pontus to Rome, Rome to Corinth (when ejected from the imperial capital), then Corinth to Ephesus, and finally a return to Rome. Part of their journeying was done as companions and fellow workers of Paul, but they also seem to have worked independently of him.

In addition, Paul tells us they "risked their necks for my life"(16:4). Unfortunately, we are told nothing of what this entailed, but knowledge of their missionary work and of the risks they took on behalf of Paul evidently was widespread in the Gentile churches, for Paul subsequently declares that to them "not only I give thanks but also all the churches of the Gentiles" (16:4). Finally, as in Ephesus (1 Corinthians 16:19), Prisca hosted a church in the couple's house in Rome (16:5). Unfortunately, we lack solid evidence regarding the relationship that obtained between hosts (Prisca and Aquila) and those who met in their house, for example, whether the host(s) enjoyed precedence and authority in the community. The answer depends on how these Christians understood their organization: if as a household, then the head of the household would be expected to exercise authority over the group;[86] if as a voluntary association structured according to the patron-client relationship, then well-to-do members who acted as hosts probably expected the community to return the favor in some way such as bestowal of honor upon their patron.

Finally, still another woman of the Christian past deserves "resurrection" from the "burial" to which a scribal error subjected her. Verse 7 includes two names, the second of which could be either masculine (*Junias*) or feminine (*Junia*).[87] Until quite recently, major translations rendered it "Junias,"[88] even though to date the masculine name is unattested in Greek and Latin literature and inscriptions, whereas the feminine *Junia* is amply in evidence. Recent scholarship, however, has accepted *Junia* as the preferred reading and regards the name *Junias* as a clerical error introduced into the manuscript tradition by a scribe, probably on the assumption that women could not (or should not) be apostles. Fortunately, the resulting "sex-change-by-translation" (Castelli's phrase) is now being reversed, as in the NAB and NRSV. It is worth noting that the recent rendering of the text enjoys the support of some sixteen commentators of the first Christian millennium.[89] Indeed, John Chrysostom lavishes praise upon Junia: "It is certainly a great thing to be an apostle; but to be outstanding among the apostles—think what praise that is! She was outstanding in her works, in her good deeds; oh, and how great is the philosophy of this woman, that she was regarded as worthy to be counted among the apostles!"[90]

Paul further describes Junia and Andronicus as "my relatives" (or "my kinsmen"), indicating that Junia, like Prisca, was a Jew. The last words of the verse ("they were in Christ before I was") indicate that she and her husband had become Christians even before Paul, which would place them among some of the earliest believers. As Jews with Greek names, both may have been freedpersons. Junia and Andronicus are also called *apostles*, a term which in Pauline usage designates a special class of *diakonoi* ("ministers"), those who do the same work of preaching and teaching but are distinguished by the claim of a direct, divine commission.[91] The designation applied to the couple thus suggests they were numbered among the larger group of apostles to whom the risen Christ appeared (1 Corinthians 15:7). As its Greek derivation ("one sent") suggests, the title refers to those sent forth as authorized evangelists. Here we have, then, another instance of the missionary partnerships (Prisca and Aquila, Euodia and Syntyche) that seem to have been common practice among early Christians.

Junia and her husband are also singled out by Paul as "prominent" or "outstanding among the apostles." His assessment is probably based on their suffering imprisonment for the sake of the Gospel, which Paul takes care to mention. Paul understood the apostolic career, his own included, as a mimesis or imitation of the crucified Christ raised by God from death; therefore, the mark of true apostleship, in Paul's view, was not eloquent speech and mighty pneumatic displays, but patient endurance of the hardships and sufferings missionary work could entail (1 Corinthians 4:8–13; 2 Corinthians 11–12). Junia and Andronicus, having suffered imprisonment, fulfilled these criteria, so Paul singled them out as "outstanding among the apostles."

Although Junia is the only woman explicitly designated *apostle* in the New Testament, she is not the only New Testament woman regarded as an apostle in early Christian literature. Origen, for example, refers to the Samaritan woman at the well (John 4:4–42) as an apostle and evangelist, as did Theophylact, archbishop of Bulgaria, centuries later.[92] That Mary Magdalene and the other women who were the first resurrection witnesses were regarded as apostles is evidenced by Hippolytus, bishop of Rome, who wrote, "Lest the female apostles doubt the angels, Christ himself came to them so that women would be apostles of Christ.... Christ showed himself to the (male) apostles and said to them:...'It is I who appeared to these women and I who wanted to send them to you as apostles.'"[93] Likewise Thecla, of the much-read apocryphal *Acts of Paul and Thecla,* was accorded the title *apostle* in *The Works of the Holy Apostle and Martyr of Christ, Thecla,* a fifth-century hagiographical writing.[94] It is worth noting that the ancient Church evidently felt free to regard various women as apostles and did so, even in the absence of their designation as such in the Gospels.

Conclusion

"Women have constituted the most spectacular casualty of history." Therefore, we should not assume that the women glimpsed in the New Testament accurately represent the proportion of women to men in the Jesus movement and early communities or their total contribution to the beginnings of Christianity. The fragments of information examined here are, we suspect, but the tip of the iceberg, with only the most prominent women of the early Christian missionary movement visible on the surface, the unknown Masses below. Among the latter are the countless women who remained in the home, making their contributions in quite conventional ways: caring for husband and children as wife and mother and dutifully managing the household, providing food and hospitality to Jesus and his disciples and, later, to traveling Christians like Paul and Phoebe. Conventional behavior, however, is by no means inconsequential behavior, for these women, by evangelizing their children and other members of the household and by providing hospitality to missionaries, played a crucial role in the transmission of faith and the spread of the Christian movement.

Other women, far fewer in numbers, we may suspect, moved beyond the walls of their own homes and so beyond the boundaries prescribed for them by the dominant culture's gender code. Among them were women who headed households and brought their households with them into the Church; others who gained prominence in the community through their patronage or their exercise of charismatic gifts; still others who traveled from village to village and later, city to city, accompanied by missionary partners. Some assumed in the churches the same roles as men: itinerant evangelist, prophet, teacher, minister or deacon. Although we lack precise information about the exact duties attached to each of these roles, one thing is clear: women's inclusion in the crucial tasks of the mission appears accepted as a matter of course. Like their male counterparts, women worked hard in the mission, and their collective efforts bore fruits for the generations that followed.

The remarkable equivalence of men's and women's roles and activities evident in the early Pauline communities was soon contested, however, and so short-lived. Efforts to restrict the public speech and activities of women are visible already in later New Testament texts, for example, 1 Timothy 2:11–15, and persist to our own time. But that is a story for another day. Fortunately, as the remainder of today's presentations will amply attest, prohibitions and restrictions have never managed to squelch the indomitable and gifting Spirit that dwells as surely in women as in men, and so what has been dubbed "the greatest story never told," the history of women, will require a substantial chapter on the women who have gone before us in the Christian churches. Women may only now be making it into "History," the recorded past; but women were indeed making "history" at the dawn of Christianity and ever after. The rising of the women to visibility in our mindscapes and imaginations is underway at last. Good news indeed—with still more to come.

NOTES

28. Arthur Schlesinger, Jr., "Introduction," in Joanna Stratton, *Pioneer Women: Voices from the Kansas Frontier* (NY: Simon and Schuster, 1981), 11.

29. The distinction between History, the recorded past, and history, all the events of the past as recollected by human beings, is made by historian Gerda Lerner in her *The Creation of Patriarchy* (NY: Oxford University Press, 1986), 4.

30. A phrase from Emmanuel Le Roy Ladurie, cited in Schlesinger, "Introduction," 11.

31. The crucial literary sources are androcentric, i.e., they assume the male as the norm, and elitist, focusing solely on the powerful few. Consequently, they give the lion's share of attention to what the elite men of power were doing. Material that illumines the lives of women and nonelite men is sorely lacking. Moreover, much of the literary material is not descriptive but prescriptive, revealing more about a male author's or patriarchal culture's desires, fantasies, and ideals than the reality of women's lives. Due to the relative unreliability of the literary sources, scholars working on the historical reality of women are studying the abundant epigraphic and papyrological materials that

shed light on women's reality. See e.g., Ute E. Eisen, *Women Officeholders in Early Christianity: Epigraphical and Literary Studies*; tr., Linda M. Maloney (Collegeville: Liturgical Press, 2000); also Kevin Madigan and Carolyn Osiek, eds. & trs., *Ordained Women in the Early Church: A Documentary History* (Baltimore: The Johns Hopkins University Press, 2005).

32. The earliest Christian woman's voice we can recover is the martyr Perpetua, whose account of her trial is included in the Martyrdom of Saints Perpetua and Felicitas; for an English translation see Ross Kraemer (ed.), *Maenads, Martyrs, Matrons, Monastics: A Sourcebook on Women's Religions in the Greco-Roman World* (Philadelphia: Fortress, 1988) 96-107. On the few early Christian texts affording access to women's own voices and experience, see M. Alexandre, "Early Christian Women," in Pauline S. Pantel (ed.), *A History of Women in the West. Vol. I. From Ancient Goddesses to Christian Saints* (Cambridge: Harvard University Press, 1992) 409-444, esp. 412. For a discussion of the challenges of writing the history of early Christian women, see esp. B. Brooten, "Early Christian Women and Their Cultural Context: Issues of Method in Historical Reconstruction," in Adela Yarbro Collins (ed.), *Feminist Perspectives on Biblical Scholarship* (Chico, California: Scholars Press, 1985), 65-91.

33. The Gospels are not written in accord with the canons of modern historiography. They reflect, rather, a complex combination of historical reminiscences and faith convictions. Therefore, one cannot simply assume that the way in which an evangelist understands or uses these designations accurately reflects the reality of the Jesus movement some forty to seven years prior.

34. For the historical-critical examination of the concept of apostle, see J.B. Lightfoot, *The Epistle of St. Paul to the Galatians* (Grand Rapids: Eerdmans, 1957) 92-101; also Hans Dieter Betz, "Apostle," in *Anchor Bible Dictionary*, Vol. I, ed., David N. Freedman (NY: Doubleday, 1992), 309-311.

35. *Disciple* is frequent in all four Gospels: 46 occurrences in Mark, 72 in Matthew, 37 in Luke, 78 in John, but absent from the rest of the New Testament, with the exception of Acts; on this, see John Meier, *A Marginal Jew: Rethinking the Historical Jesus. Vol. 3. Companions and Competitors* (NY: Doubleday, 2001), 41. The term *apostle* occurs 79 times in the New Testament, of which 68 are in Luke and Paul; see Lightfoot, *Epistle*, 94.

36. Research has established that the term *apostle* was variously understood and applied in the first Christian decades and that it was not restricted to the twelve men who constituted a symbolically significant inner circle around the historical Jesus (the regathering of the twelve tribes of Israel) and whom he envisioned as exercising a particular role in the coming reign of God. The popular tendency to equate disciples, apostles, and the Twelve and the mistaken reduction of the *apostles* to *the Twelve* are due mainly to Luke, whose account of the selection of the Twelve (Luke 6:13; also Matthew 10:1-2) suggests that out of a larger group of "disciples" Jesus "chose twelve, whom he also named apostles." Yet Luke never uses the phrase *the Twelve Apostles* in his Gospel or in Acts, and in the latter refers to Barnabas and Paul as apostles (14:4, 14; see also 13:2-3). Thus, although Luke uses the designations *the Twelve* and *the apostles* interchangeably, his restriction of *apostle* to *the Twelve* is not ironclad. As we will see below (Part III), post–New Testament writers did not feel constrained by the Lukan inclination to restrict the term to the Twelve. Rather, their designation of particular women as apostles reflects the broader understanding of *apostle* evident in Pauline literature, including the pre-Pauline tradition cited in 1 Corinthians 15:3–9 which, in listing those to whom the risen Christ appeared, identifies Cephas, the Twelve, and what is obviously a larger category, "all the apostles."

37. Meier, *Marginal Jew*, 126.

38. Meier, *Marginal Jew*, 126.

39. Not all scholars conclude that the institution of the Twelve originated with Jesus. For a list of those who think it probable that the Twelve arose not during Jesus' mission but in the early Church, see Meier, *Marginal Jew*, 128. I remain persuaded that Jesus created the Twelve during his public ministry and that they were twelve men. For the arguments, see *Marginal Jew*, 128–147.

40. That the women's sudden presence at the cross, for which there is no preparation in the preceding narrative, is not required by Mark's narrative logic suggests the historicity of their travels with Jesus and their presence at the crucifixion.

41. It is widely agreed, given Luke's well-known apologetic concern to present Christianity as a respectable religion, that this depiction of women moving about rural Galilee with an unmarried man and at least 12 other men is hardly something the evangelist would have invented.

42. Because in Greek the masculine plural may be interpreted inclusively unless the context indicates otherwise, it is possible that the masculine grammatical form for "disciples" referred to female as well as male disciples. However, the evangelists' occasional use of the term "the women" (*gynaikes*, Matthew 27:55; 28:5; Mark 15:40, 41; Luke 8:2; 23:27,49,55; 24:5,10,22,24) may be read as in effect distinguishing them as *other* than "the disciples." Alternatively, it is also possible that precisely because the Greek for *disciples* is a masculine form, when an evangelist had in mind the actions of women of the discipleship group, it was necessary to introduce the term *the women* simply to single them out from the men of the group. Therefore, use of the phrase *the women* in and of itself does not prove that the term *the disciples* (*hoi mathētai*) was necessarily exclusive of women.

43. Luise Schottroff, e.g., proposes, "The fact that women as disciples of Jesus are not mentioned in the texts that can be traced back to the Jesus movement of Palestine can be explained by the androcentrism of language and the 'equality' that poverty produces," and further observes, "The different situation of women and men is not an issue in the Jesus movement of Palestine since experience is determined by the equality that poverty and the common hope of God's kingdom produce"; see her *Let the Oppressed Go Free: Feminist Perspectives on the New Testament* (Louisville: Westminster/John Knox Press, 1993) 92-93, 97. I find no evidence for the proposal by some that it was the widely known historical memory of women traveling with Jesus that forced the evangelists to include this tradition, but that they deliberately obscured the women's discipleship by denying them the title *disciples* and deliberately omitting stories of their call.

44. Among the reconstructions proposed by Historical Jesus research, Jesus as a miracle-working prophet like Elijah is, to my mind, the most compelling. In presenting himself to Israel as an Elijah-like eschatological prophet, not surprisingly, like his predecessor, Jesus called some individuals to leave their ordinary work and families behind to join in his itinerant mission of proclaiming the coming reign of God. The similarity between the story of Elijah's call of Elisha (1 Kings 19:19-21) and the call stories in the Gospels, each involving men, is widely recognized.

45. Luke's description of the women who traveled with Jesus and the Twelve is perhaps instructive. That "some women who had been cured of evil spirits and infirmities" and "Mary, called Magdalene, from whom seven demons had gone out," physically accompanied Jesus on the road may suggest that women who were healed by Jesus experienced this as equivalent to a call of call to follow him. Although this cannot be established, the fact that the cure of blind Bartimaeus results in him following Jesus "on the way" (Mark 10:46-52) adds to the plausibility of the suggestion. It may be that persons joined Jesus' movement by different routes, some based on a verbal call by the prophet, others drawn in by their experience of the healing power of the coming reign of God proclaimed by Jesus.

46. Meier, *Marginal Jew*, 78. One might well ask, does not the lack of a term for "female disciple" in fact prove that women were not disciples? Meier remarks, "One is reminded here of the danger of doing either history or theology simply through word-studies. New realities emerge on the historical scene before there are new words to describe them, and sometimes the time lag between new reality and new coinage is lengthy" (78-79). Some fifty plus years after Jesus' public ministry, the sole New Testament occurrence of the feminine form *mathetria* appears in Acts 9:36 to describe Tabitha.

47. Meier, *Marginal Jew*, 79.

48. Hence, the charge that Jesus ate with tax collectors and sinners (Mark 2:17). On this, see Corley, *Women and the Historical Jesus. Feminist Myths of Christian Origins* (Santa Rosa, California: Polebridge Press, 2002), esp. 32-44.

49. Meier, *Marginal Jew*, 79. Meier continues, "A traveling entourage of husbandless female supporters, some of whom were former demoniacs who were now giving Jesus money or food, would only have heightened the suspicion and scandal Jesus already faced in a traditional peasant society. Yet, scandal or no scandal, Jesus allowed them to follow and serve him. Whatever the problems of vocabulary, the most probable conclusion is that Jesus viewed and treated these women as disciples" (79-80).

50. The question recently appeared as the title of a book about women's history: Rosalind Miles, *Who Cooked the Last Supper? The Women's History of the World* (NY: Three Rivers Press, 2001).

51. Scholarship makes a distinction between the Last Supper as historical event and the Gospel representations of that historical event, which may or may not be historically accurate or accurate to a degree. It is well to remember that the earliest account of the Last Supper (Mark) was written some forty years after the actual event; hence, the necessity of an inquiry as to its historical accuracy.

52. See Kathleen E. Corley, *Private Women, Public Meals: Social Conflict in the Synoptic Tradition* (Peabody: Hendrickson Publishers, 1993); Dorothy A. Lee, "Presence or Absence? The Question of Women Disciples at the Last Supper," in Suzanne Scholz (ed.), *Biblical Studies Alternatively: An Introductory Reader* (Upper Saddle River, NJ: Prentice Hall, 2003) 121-136; Robert J. Karris, *Eating Your Way Through Luke's Gospel* (Collegeville: Liturgical Press, 2006) esp. 85-87, 90-94. On the presence of women in Luke's Last Supper scene, see Quentin Quesnell, "The Women at Luke's Supper," in *Political Issues in Luke-Acts*, ed., Richard J. Cassidy and Philip Scharper (Maryknoll, NY: Orbis, 1983), 59-79.

53. The verb *diakoneō* is variously translated "to wait on (at table)," "to serve," "to minister." The occurrences of forms of the verb *diakoneō* elsewhere in Mark (1:13; 1:31; 10:45) clearly evoke the image of serving food, and do so in 15:40-41. For a thorough discussion of the various meanings of this and related Greek terms, see John N. Collins, *Diakonia: Re-interpreting the Ancient Sources* (NY: Oxford University Press, 1990).

54. Historical Jesus scholars agree that the Jesus movement practiced inclusive table fellowship. In her *Private Women, Public Meals*, Corley sets Jesus' practice in the context of the "convivial inclusivity" practiced by a variety of religious and philosophical groups in the Hellenistic world, and in so doing, has detected the presence of women at Jesus' table: "At an early layer of the Gospel tradition Jesus is slandered for his table practice, which includes the presence of 'tax-collectors and sinners' for meals, and features 'wine-bibbing' and 'gluttony.' Such characterizations reflect stereotypical slander used against those known for dining with 'promiscuous' or 'liberated' women. Other religious and philosophical groups were criticized in like manner for including women in socially mixed public meals" (184).

55. Corley cites evidence for the presence of women and children at the Passover meal; see *Private Women, Public Meals*, esp. 69, 71.

56 Lee, "Presence or Absence," 134-135.

57. See Corley, *Private Women, Public Meals*, esp. 66-75, 180-186.

58. In these scenes, it is the woman's personal status (a sinner, Luke 7:39) or her waste of resources (costly ointment, Mark 14:4-5; Matthew 26:8-9; John 12:4-5), not her gender, that Jesus' table fellows find objectionable.

59. Regardless of whether we can ever know exactly who ate the Last Supper with the historical Jesus, it is worth noting that the earliest Gospel account of the Last Supper, Mark's, need not be read as compelling the conclusion that only Jesus and the Twelve were present. Indeed, the Markan account of the Last Supper, which does not identify the two disciples sent to prepare for the meal (14:12-16) as men, permits us to imagine a scene in which Jesus and the Twelve men who arrive with him once all is ready (14:17) join at least the two disciples who had made the preparations, nothing indicating that the two disciples departed or were dismissed. In fact, Jesus' remark shortly thereafter, "It is one of the Twelve, one who is dipping bread into the bowl with me" (14:20), presupposes the presence of others in the room. Moreover, since the Markan narrative does not require that we read "disciples" as referring only to men (see above n. 15), then we may imagine the two disciples as two of the women who, according to 15:40-41, had been engaged in *diēkonoun* and accompanied him to Jerusalem. Thus, regardless of what one concludes about the historical question, Mark's Gospel may be read as scriptural foundation for a revised, more inclusive scene in the Christian imagination. For an example, see n. 35 below.

60. Corley, *Women and the Historical Jesus*, 52.

61. Recently some artists have rendered the Gospel scene quite differently from the exclusively male affair with which we Christians are familiar. In an obvious variation on the Da Vinci painting, Mary Lynn Sheetz depicts a group of twelve women around the table, identifying them as, e.g.,

Mary of Nazareth, Thea Bowman, Theresa of Avila, Dorothy Day, among others; see "Women's Work" at www.alterni-tee.com/womensworkposter.htm. I prefer, however, Bohdan Piasecki's "Last Supper" (Poland, 1998), which depicts not only Christ and the twelve men but also six women and two children. Piasecki's rendering permits us to imagine a Passover ritual celebrated by Jesus with his "family" of those "brothers, sisters, and mothers who do the will of God" (Mark 3:35). For Piasecki's "Last Supper," visit www.christianartfromireland.com.

62. Mark 15:40; 15:47; 16:1; 16:9; Matt. 27:55-56; 27:61; 28:1; Luke 8:2; 24:10; John 19:25; 20:1; 20:11-18.

63. Although the ancients believed that powerful forces, which they personified and called "demons," could enter and take possession of human beings, many modern Christians do not include such beings in their cosmology. A number of social-scientific disciplines consider possession to be a problem of the relationship between a person and society, e.g., as a protest against injustices of various kinds. For an intriguing application of social-scientific theory to the demon possession of Mary Magdalene and to Jesus' exorcistic activity, see Carmen Bernabé Ubieta, "Mary Magdalene and the Seven Demons in Social-Scientific Perspective," in Ingrid Rosa Kitzberger, ed., *Transformative Encounters: Jesus and Women Re-Viewed* (Leiden: Brill, 2000) 203-223. In investigating the meaning and significance of Mary's Magdalene's possession, it should be noted that apparently Jesus was perceived by some as possessed (Mark 3:22).

64. For an enlightening discussion of ancient assumptions about poor or lower-class women, including associations with prostitution and demon possession, see Corley, *Women and the Historical Jesus*, esp. 32-43.

65. On Mary Magdalene, see Holly E. Hearon, *The Mary Magdalene Tradition: Witness and Counter-Witness in Early Christian Communities* (Collegeville, MN: Liturgical Press, 2004); Carla Ricci, *Mary Magdalene and Many Others: Women Who Followed Jesus* (Minneapolis: Fortress Press, 1994); Susan Haskins, Mary Magdalene. Myth and Metaphor (NY: Harcourt Brace and Co., 1993); Jane Schaberg, The Resurrection of Mary Magdalene. Legends, Apocrypha, and the Christian Testament (NY: Continuum, 2003); Ann G. Brock, Mary Magdalene. The First Apostle: The Struggle for Authority, Harvard Theological Studies 51 (Cambridge: Harvard University Press, 2003); Ingrid Maisch, Mary Magdalene. The Image of a Woman Through the Centuries (Collegeville, MN: Liturgical Press, 1998).

66. The numerous art images of Mary Magdalene as a sensuous sinful woman and penitent prostitute, a rendering without basis in the biblical text, have proved nearly indelible in the Christian imagination. For an introduction to Mary Magdalene in Western art, see Jane Lahr, *Searching for Mary Magdalene: A Journey Through Art and Literature* (NY: Welcome Books, 2006); also, Diane Apostolos-Cappadona, *In Search of Mary Magdalene: Images and Traditions* (NY: American Bible Society, 2002). In marked and refreshing contrast are the images of contemporary artists, Louis S. Glanzman and Janet McKenzie. To see Mr. Glanzman's renderings of Mary Magdalene and other biblical women, see Edwina Gateley and Louis S. Glanzman, *Soul Sisters: Women in Scripture Speak to Women Today* (Maryknoll, NY: Orbis Books, 2002) or visit www.louisglanzman.com. For Janet McKenzie's images of Mary Magdalene, which includes a triptych entitled "The Succession of Mary Magdalene," visit www.janetmckenzie.com.

67. For a translation of the pertinent section of Gregory's sermon, see Karen L. King, *The Gospel of Mary of Magdala: Jesus and the First Woman Apostle* (Santa Rosa, CA: Polebridge Press, 2003), 151.

68. One witnesses this gradual eclipse of Mary's role as "apostle to the apostles" in the history of art. A survey of her iconography in Western Christian art demonstrates that the earliest depictions of Mary Magdalene were as the first witness of the resurrection. Later, however, the confusion with the unnamed sinful woman of Luke 7:36-50 becomes apparent, as ointment jars, long-flowing hair, bare shoulders or breast, and tears become routine in representations.

69. Wayne Meeks, *The First Urban Christians. The Social World of the Apostle Paul* (New Haven: Yale University Press, 1983), 55-63.

70. Prophecy flourished in the Church for centuries, including among its women; see David Aune, *Prophecy in Early Christianity and the Ancient Mediterranean World* (Grand Rapids: Eerdmans, 1992).

71. Even if Paul's words contradict his stance in 11:2-16, the behavior implied by these verses is consistent with the pneumatic fervor and freedom that members of the community, including its women prophets, experienced.

72. See Ben Witherington, *Conflict and Community in Corinth: A Socio-Rhetorical Commentary on 1 and 2 Corinthians* (Grand Rapids: Eerdmans, 1995), 287, who continues, "it is very believable that these women assumed that Christian prophets or prophetesses functioned much like the oracle at Delphi, who only prophesied in response to questions." For an engaging reconstruction of the identity and activities of these women, see Antoinette Clark Wire, *The Corinthian Women Prophets: A Reconstruction Through Paul's Rhetoric* (Minneapolis: Fortress, 1990).

73. Margaret Mitchell, *Paul and the Rhetoric of Reconciliation: An Exegetical Investigation of the Language and Composition of 1 Corinthians* (Louisville: Westminster/John Knox, 1992), 279. The very nature of ecstatic experiences meant that anyone could have them and that they were not under the control of an external party. Close reading of 1 Corinthians 11-14 reveals that the Corinthian community, with its ample spiritual gifts, presented a trying pastoral challenge for Paul, who also valued "peace" and "order" (1 Corinthians 14:26-40).

74. On the women in Acts, see Ivoni Richter Reimer, *Women in the Acts of the Apostles: A Feminist Liberation Perspective* (Minneapolis: Fortress, 1995).

75. One commentator has offered the plausible suggestion that Paul's plea for unity ("be of the same mind") hints at what is at stake. According to Roman legal traditions, the equal partnership (*societas*) into which the Philippians and Paul had entered was operative as long as the partners "are...'of the same mind' about the centrality of the purpose around which the partnership was formed in the first place." Apparently that partnership was in some way jeopardized by the strife between Euodia and Syntyche. On this, see J.P. Sampley, *Pauline Partnership in Christ* (Philadelphia: Fortress, 1980) 62-63.

76. E. Earle Ellis, "Paul and His Co-workers," *New Testament Studies* 17 (1971) 437-52, esp. 440-41. Later evidence indicates that women continued to be active in the post-Pauline Churches of Philippi. That is unsurprising in view of what we know of women's patronage and their civic and religious activities in the region. Study of inscriptional evidence reveals that well-to-do women maintained temples, sponsored festivals, and acted as priestesses. Given this cultural heritage, it is unlikely that the growing Christian community, if it hoped to attract these women, accustomed as they were to prominent roles in pagan cults, could deny them a comparable prominence in their newly adopted religion. See Ross Kramer, *Her Share of the Blessings: Women's Religions among Pagans, Jews, and Christians in the Greco-Roman World* (NY: Oxford University Press, 1992), 80-92. For discussion of the leadership of women in Second Temple Judaism, see Bernadette J. Brooten, *Women Leaders in the Ancient Synagogue: Inscriptional Evidence and Background Issues* (Chico, CA: Scholars Press, 1982).

77. A recent study has offered the intriguing suggestion that "...the importance of Euodia and Syntyche...in the context of the whole appeal for unity in the letter may suggest that these two women are among the *episkopoi*, probably leaders of local house Churches" (Madigan and Osiek, *Ordained Women*, 11). The term *episkopoi* , which Paul uses in tandem with *diakonoi* in Phil. 1:1, may be translated "bishops." There is a consensus, however, that at this early stage of the Christian movement, the term did not yet mean "bishop" as we know it. Therefore, in Phil. 1:1, *episkopoi* is more properly rendered "overseers," as in the New American Bible. Thus, to suggest that Euodia and Syntyche might have been *episkopoi* is not to claim they were "bishops," but rather, "overseers" of some kind in the Philippian community.

78. Whether this chapter actually belonged originally to this letter or to another is a textual issue that need not concern us. Insofar as the chapter is considered authentically Pauline, and so reflects the life of Pauline communities, the textual issue does not affect what this chapter reveals about women in first century Christian communities. On Romans 16, see esp. Elisabeth Schüssler Fiorenza, "Missionaries, Apostles, Coworkers: Romans 16 and the Reconstruction of Women's Early Christian History," *Word and World* 6 (1986) 420-433; Elizabeth A. Castelli, "Romans," in *Searching the Scriptures*, Vol. II, Elisabeth Schüssler Fiorenza, ed. (NY: Crossroad, 1994) 276-280; Bonnie Thurston, "Women in the New Testament: The Example of Romans 16," in *Scripture as the Soul of Theology*, Edward J. Mahoney, ed. (Collegeville, MN: Liturgical Press, 2005), 40-59.

79. The term *co-worker* or *fellow worker* does not mean that these women (or men similarly desig-nated) were Paul's "helpers" or "assistants." Only five coworkers (Erastus, Mark, Timothy, Titus, Tychicus) "stand in explicit subordination to Paul, serving him or being subject to his instructions"; see Ellis, "Paul and His Co-workers," 439.

80. The later term *diakonissa* first appears in a datable Greek text in Canon 19; see Madigan and Osiek, *Ordained Women*, 8.

81. Ellis, "Paul and His Co-workers," 441-442.

82. Paul's reference to Phoebe as *diakonos* has the important implication "that whatever the func-tion of a *diakonos* in a first-century Pauline Church, in the early years any reference to *diakonoi* as a group must not be understood necessarily to refer only to men. Therefore, it is questionable whether references to *diakonoi* in Phil 1:1 or the Letters of Ignatius have in view only men" (Ma-digan and Osiek, *Ordained Women*, 4). 1 Timothy 3:11 may be further evidence that women were *diakonoi*, although scholars remain divided on whether the women mentioned are *diakonoi* or wives of *diakonoi*. The particular usage of *diakonos* in 1 Timothy, written between fifty or sixty years after Romans, indicates that the role, like that of *episkopos*, had evolved into an institutional office of some kind, hence, the translation preferable in this case, "deacon."

83. See Ramsay MacMullen, "Women in Public in the Roman Empire," *Historia* 29 (1980) 211; also Van Bremen, *The Limits of Participation* (n.32 above); and Meeks, *First Urban Christians*, 24-5.

84. Robert Jewett, "Paul, Phoebe, and the Spanish Mission," in *The Social World of Formative Chris-tianity and Judaism*, J. Neusner et al., eds. (Philadelphia: Fortress, 1988), 142-161; see esp. 153.

85. It has been objected that women's contributions would have been severely hampered by their illiteracy. However, because the earliest believers in Christ relied heavily on oral tradition for the transmission of Gospel tradition, women would have had to acquire little if any literacy to be ac-tive participants in the transmission and interpretation of traditions about Jesus. See Kraemer, *Her Share of the Blessings*, 144. John Chrysostom celebrated Priscilla's outstanding activity as a missionary artisan in his *Salutate Priscillam et Aquilam* 2.1. In contrast, Tertullian's praise of only Aquila probably represents an early attempt to demote Priscilla (and women who might be inspired by her precedent) from prominence (Reimer, *Women in the Acts of the Apostles*, 216).

86. Meeks, *First Urban Christians*, 76.

87. Depending on how it is accented in the manuscripts, *Junian* is either the accusative of the masculine *Junias* or the accusative of the feminine *Junia*. On the history of interpretation of Rom. 16:7 and on the manuscript issues, see Bernadette Brooten, "Junia—Outstanding Among the Apostles (Rom. 16:7)" in *Women Priests: A Catholic Commentary on the Vatican Declaration* (NY: Paulist Press, 1977), 141-14; and more recently Eldon Jay Epp, *Junia. The First Woman Apostle* (Minneapolis: Fortress, 2005).

88. Among major English translations, six translate the name as "Junias," male (RSV, NASB, NEB, GN, NIV, NJB), and three translate it as "Junia," female (KJV, NAB, NRSV). To compare English translations, see *The Precise Parallel New Testament*, ed., J.R. Kohlenberger III (NY: Oxford Uni-versity Press, 1995).

89. For a list, see Epp, *Junia*, 32.

90. From his commentary on Romans 31.2; translation cited in Eisen, *Women Officeholders*, 48.

91. Ellis, "Paul and His Co-workers," 444-45. In reference to his own apostolic labors, Paul refers to himself as *diakonos* (1 Corinthians 3:5), thereby evidencing the close relationship between the two terms.

92. Eisen, *Women Officeholders*, 50.

93. Hippolytus, *De Cantico* 24-26, cited in Brock, *Mary Magdalene*, 1-2.

94. For a reading of the *Acts of Paul and Thecla*, see Susan Calef, "Thecla 'Tried and True' and the Inversion of Romance," in *A Feminist Companion to the New Testament Apocrypha*, Amy-Jill Levine, ed., (London & NY: T & T Clark, 2006), 163-185.

3. Women in the Early Church: A Portrait Gallery

William Harmless, SJ, PhD, Professor of Theology
Creighton University

To be a Church historian means serving the Church's sometimes fragile and neglected memory. Most pastoral ministers are rightly occupied with serving the demanding day-to-day needs of the people of God. Theirs is a calling both noble and exhausting. Few have the time or energy to enter into this intricate enterprise of Church history, this deep remembering that seeks to tap into the vast recesses and much-neglected archives of the Church's memory, that seeks to salvage its sometimes great and forgotten depths of wisdom as well as its sometimes ignominious catalogue of misdeeds and painful shortsightedness.

The danger of institutional forgetfulness is real. The risk is that we suffer a collective institutional amnesia. I want to thank all of you for coming together today, for taking some time to explore the extraordinary contributions of women over the centuries, to cull from those centuries some small measure of a hard-won wisdom. My focus here will be on the patristic period: from the end of the New Testament to roughly the year 600.

Women in the Roman World: Snapshots

If you decided to investigate the biography of one of the most famous Christian women of our time, Blessed Mother Teresa of Calcutta (1910–1997), you would look not only at the facts of her life but also at the multiethnic culture she was raised in—namely, Albania under the old Ottoman Empire—as well as the intricate, many-sided culture where she spent much of her working career: India. This same sensitivity to context is required to understand early Christian women. So I want to begin with a few, quick snapshots of the lives of women in the ancient world.

Over the last fifty years, extraordinary work has been done by scholars, both women and men, who have translated and analyzed a vast welter of data, not only from long-neglected texts in Greek and Latin, but also from materials in other ancient languages such as Coptic, Syriac, Armenian, and Ethiopic. These materials include inscriptions on monuments and tombstones and coins, letters preserved on scraps of ancient papyri, and much, much else.[95] They give us small but intriguing glimpses of what the ancient world actually looked like at ground level. From this miscellany of sources, I have assembled a few snapshots of women's life in the ancient world.

Let me begin with an inscription from a physician who composed a homage to his wife, who was also a physician. This is what he had carved at her burial site:

> *Farewell, lady Panthia, from your husband. After your departure, I keep up my lasting grief for your cruel death. Hera, goddess of marriage, never saw such a wife: your beauty, your wisdom, your chastity. You bore me children completely like myself; you cared for your bridegroom and your children; you guided straight the rudder of life in our home and raised high our common fame in healing—though you were a woman, you were not behind me in skill. In recognition of this, your bridegroom Glycon built this tomb for you. I also buried here the body of [my father] immortal Philadelphius, and I myself will lie here when I die, since with you alone I shared my bed when I was alive, so may I cover myself in the ground that we share.[96]*

A second snapshot: This comes from Saint Jerome (circa 347–420) who, despite his fame as a biblical scholar, had a stern distaste for marriage and family life and was no less famous for his wicked gift for satire. Here is his description of housekeeping in the ancient world:

> *Over there, the babies are prattling, the children hang on her for kisses, the accounts are being added up, and the money got ready for payment. Here, a posse of cooks, girded for action, is pounding meat, and a crowd of weaving-women chattering. Then a message comes that her husband has brought his friends home. She circles the rooms like a swallow: Is the couch smooth? Have they swept the floor? Are the cups properly set out? Is dinner ready? Tell me, where in all this is the thought of God?[97]*

Then as now, women did not simply manage busy households. We get these ever-so-faint glimpses of the lives of working-class women from the brief inscriptions found on their tombs. Many of these women were diligent and hard-working, often poor or slaves, many dying young. For example:

> *To Italia, dressmaker of Cocceia Phyllis. She lived 20 years. Acastus, her fellow slave, put this up because she was poor.*

To the gods of the dead. Polydeuces dedicated this to the well-deserving Cypare, a hairdresser.

To the gods of the dead. [The tomb] of Irene the wool-weigher. She lived 28 years. Olympus put this up for his well-deserving wife.

To the gods of the dead. To Abudia Megiste, freedwoman of Marcus, most kindly, Marcus Abudius Luminaris, her patron and husband, built [this tomb] for the well-deserving dealer in grains and vegetables from the middle staircase....

Sacred to the gods of the dead. To Hapaste, a Greek stenographer, who lived 25 years. Pittosus put this up for his sweetest wife.[98]

Another portrait comes from Saint John Chrysostom (circa 347–407). Chrysostom grew up in Antioch and eventually served at the turn of the fifth century as bishop of Constantinople, where he earned wide acclaim for his eloquence. (*Chrysostom* is a later nickname that means "golden-mouth"). His father had been a high-ranking officer in the Roman military who, as you will hear, died when Chrysostom was quite young. In the following account, Chrysostom recounts his mother's experience as a widow and a single mother raising a young son:

Sitting close by me on the bed on which she had given me birth, she burst into tears, and then spoke words more touching than the tears. And this was her sad complaint: 'My child,' she said, 'I was not for long permitted to enjoy your father's virtues, for so it pleased God. His death followed very soon after my travail over you, and left you an orphan and me a widow before any time, with all the burdens of widowhood, which only those who have borne them can properly understand. No words could describe the stormy sea which a young girl faces, if she has only just left her father's house without any experience of the world, and is suddenly struck with unbearable sorrow and compelled to shoulder cares too great for her years and her sex. For, as I know too well, she has to correct the carelessness of servants, to guard against their misconduct, to thwart the schemes of relatives, and to bear with dignity the insults of public officials and their rudeness about payments of taxes. And if her dead husband should have left a child, even when that child is a girl, she will cause great anxiety to her mother, though not expense and fear. But a son fills her with a host of misgivings every day that passes, and even more anxieties. I say nothing of the heavy expenditure she must incur if she wants to bring him up as a gentleman. Still, none of these thoughts persuaded me to contract a second marriage and to introduce another husband to your father's house. No, I remained patient, while troubles surged around me, and I did not flinch from the iron furnace of widowhood. My chief help was from above. And I found great consolation in those trials in gazing continually at your face and treasuring in you a living and exact image of my dead husband. So while you were still a baby and had not even learnt to speak, at the time when children give most pleasure to their parents, you afforded me great comfort.[99]

Another snapshot—and it is an anguishing one. Abortion is one of the great moral battles of our world. In the ancient world, there was another, no-less-serious reality: infanticide, the leaving of babies to die of exposure. Here is an example, a startling letter preserved on a papyrus that dates from the time of Jesus' birth:

Hilarion to Alis his sister, heartiest greetings, and to my dear Berous and Apollonarion. Know that we are still even now in Alexandria. Do not worry if when all the others return I remain in Alexandria. I beg and beseech you to take care of the little child, and as soon as we receive wages I will send them to you. If—good luck to you!—you bear offspring, if it is a male, let it live; if it is a female, expose it. You told Aphrodisias, 'Do not forget me.' How can I forget you? I beg you therefore not to worry. The 29th year of Caesar, Pauni 23.[100]

This letter in its anguishing brevity captures attitudes that, to our eye, seem strangely contradictory. The author has a child for whom he cares deeply and a wife for whom he cares deeply. He is a poor, working-class man who saves and sends all his wages home to his wife, and yet, in the most offhanded, pedestrian way, simply says of their forthcoming child: "If it is a female, expose it."

Richard Miller, in his opening remarks, alluded to ancient medical theories, notably those of Aristotle. Here is a passage from another ancient medical theorist, Galen (circa 217). For Galen, as for Aristotle, women, because of a "heat deficiency," were seen as somehow less than fully human:

So too the woman is less perfect than the man in respect to the generative parts. For the parts were formed within her when she was still a fetus, but could not because of the defect in the heat emerge and project on the outside, and this, though making the animal itself that was being formed less perfect than one that is complete in all respects, provided no small advantage for the race; for there needs must be a female. Indeed, you ought not to think our creator would purposely make half the whole race imperfect and, as it were, mutilated, unless there was to be some great advantage in such a mutilation.[101]

This attitude—that women are somehow "mutilated men"—was shockingly commonplace.

This is the world early Christians moved in, or at least a glimpse into that world's ordinariness, and its differences from our own. To gain some appreciation of the lives of early Christian women, we need to savor the constraints, the prejudices, and the often narrow opportunities their world afforded them. Gillian Clark, one of the leading scholars in this field, has noted her own experience of teaching: that her theology students are "often shocked by early Christian teachings on women which were simply the cultural norm of Greco-Roman antiquity."[102] It is important that we appreciate in what ways Christian authors reflected the culture of Late Antiquity and in what ways they parted from it.

Early Christian Women: A Survey

My prime goal here is to be a storyteller, a purveyor of anecdotes about early Christian women, to illustrate the wide-ranging roles they assumed and the vocations they embraced. Some of these women you may have heard a little about, and others, nothing at all. What we know of them comes from a vast library of ancient sources dug up thanks to the hard labors of scholars of early Christianity. My approach here will be to put together a small portrait gallery. Think of these as paintings in words. To give them the kind of analysis they deserve goes far beyond what I have time for here. Therefore, in the notes that accompany this, I suggest various scholarly studies that give these women the careful attention and nuanced analysis they deserve.

1. Women as Apostles: Thecla

The most famous woman of early Christianity was a fictional character, not a historical figure: Saint Thecla. For early Christians, Thecla was *the* great female hero. Her story appears in a work called *The Acts of Paul and Thecla*.[103]

This text is classified as New Testament apocrypha, a work that purports to come from apostolic times but was, from a very early date, one whose apostolic credentials were impugned or denied. Many of these apocryphal works are simply pious fictions that date mostly from the second century. Early Christians loved to make up stories about heroic figures of the Christian past, especially to fill in gaps in the New Testament story. And just as we have romance novels today, so in the Greco-Roman world they had their romance novels. *The Acts of Paul and Thecla* is a Christian version of this common ancient genre. Its anonymous author tells various legends of this supposed female apostle, Saint Thecla. We date the work sometime prior to the year 200 because the North African theologian Tertullian (died 220) denounced it (with the vigor he denounced many things) around that time.

The work's opening scene reminds me of Shakespeare's *Romeo and Juliet*, the scene where Juliet leans out from her balcony. The author of the *Acts* portrays the teenage Thecla leaning out her window, entranced as she listens to the voice of Saint Paul preaching a sermon within earshot. This Paul is rather different from the Paul in the New Testament. This Paul preaches a sermon that mimics Jesus' Beatitudes, and its keynote is a call to celibacy, as though that were the heart of the Christian message:

> Blessed are the pure in heart, for they shall see God; blessed are those who have kept the flesh chaste, for they shall become a temple of God; blessed are the continent, for God shall speak with them; blessed are those who have kept aloof from this world, for they shall be pleasing to God; blessed are those who have wives as though not having them, for they shall experience God; blessed are those who have fear of God, for they shall become angels of God;...blessed are the bodies of virgins, for they shall be well pleasing to God and shall not lose the reward of their chastity. For the word of the Father shall become to them a work of salvation in the day of the Son, and they shall rest for ever and ever.[104]

Thecla listens and is transfixed. The sermon moves her to become a Christian. She had been engaged to be married, but because of this evangelical call to celibacy, she breaks off her engagement. Paul's preaching was a little too successful; he attracted large numbers of local women, encouraging them to abandon husbands and family. The city's authorities, therefore, arrested him, accused him of sorcery and, in the end, sent him packing. Thecla, in the meantime, endures grueling trials. She is arrested for refusing marriage. Even her mother rabidly condemns her, calling for her to be burned at the stake.

Realism is hardly a feature of ancient romance literature anymore than it is of its modern counterpart. So Thecla is arrested, tried, condemned, and led out to be executed. It is to be a death by burning. She is stripped (a standard ancient practice of public humiliation), but when the pyre's flames do not leap up and burn her, she is released. This is the first of her miraculous escapes.

Another time, she is arrested and condemned to be killed by animals. Those of you have who have seen the movie *Gladiator* have a good image of what this involved. Romans routinely made execution of their condemned prisoners a part of their public entertainments, and one popular form was to have prisoners mauled and killed by wild beasts. According to the *Acts*, Thecla has this miraculous power over animals. In one episode, a lioness not only refuses to attack her, but becomes her protector against other beasts sent to kill her.

Finally, in one famous episode, Thecla faces execution by being thrown into a pool full of seals. We may not think of seals as scary or dangerous, I realize, but the author of this work seems to have thought of them as something ferocious, something like sharks. Early on, Thecla had tried to get Paul to baptize her, but he denied her readiness. So in this late episode, Thecla announces that since she is facing death, she will just have to baptize herself and, with great bravado jumps into the seal-filled pool, saying, "In the name of Jesus Christ, I baptize myself on my last day." Her plunge and invocation causes a shock wave through the water, leaving all the seals floating on the surface, stunned.[105]

At story's end, Thecla announces her vocation to be an apostle. She wanders around Asia, seeking out Paul. For a woman to wander around alone was, of course, very dangerous. So she shaves her head and dresses as man. In the end, she reunites with Paul, who ends up sending her on an apostolic mission. Thus she would be seen in the later Christian imagination as both a martyr who didn't die and a woman apostle.

The theologian Tertullian had little sympathy for such things—women apostles and self-baptisms—and proclaimed,

In fact, concerning The Acts of Paul and Thecla, wrongly attributed to Paul, they appeal to the example of Thecla as giving women the right to teach and to baptize. Let them know that a priest in Asia constructed this document, as if he were heaping up glory for Paul by his own effort. When he was convicted and confessed that he done it out of love for Saint Paul, he lost his position as priest. But how credible will it seem that Paul gave a woman the power of teaching

and baptizing when he firmly prohibited a woman from learning
when he says, in 1 Corinthians "Let them be silent and question their
husbands at home."[106]

Tertullian's denunciation had little effect. Thecla's reputation continued to grow. Later there arose in Seleucia a popular shrine dedicated to her.[107] Pilgrims to such shrines often took home as souvenirs small *ampullae*, or oil vials. One sixth-century example portrays Thecla standing next to her symbolic protector, the lioness.[108]

2. Women as Martyrs: Perpetua

Let us shift from fiction to history. Of the famous women martyrs in the early Church, perhaps the most renowned was Saint Perpetua (died 203). She was from a prominent North African family from near Carthage (modern Tunis). At the time of her arrest, she was apparently in her early twenties, a mother with an infant son. (Interestingly, there is no mention of a husband nor any mention of her as a widow.) The document that records her final days and death is entitled *The Martyrdom of the Saints Perpetua and Felicity*.[109] It is a brief text, some twelve pages, and has three sections. The first is a prologue by an anonymous editor who emphasizes Perpetua's gifts as a visionary, seeing them as the fulfillment of the prophecy of the prophet Joel: that the old will dream dreams and the young will see visions (Joel 2:4). The middle section is Perpetua's prison diary. Written in the first person, it gives fascinating details of her feelings and inner struggles as well as accounts of her remarkable visions. The final section is an eyewitness account of her martyrdom.

Let me touch on a few facets of the text. Perpetua was martyred in the persecution of Emperor Septimus Severus. As best we can judge, it was directed not against *all* Christians, but only against new converts and the catechists who prepared them for baptism. Think about it: One way to close down a school is by closing down its admissions office. That seems to have been the Roman strategy here: shut down Christianity by shutting off the flow of new converts. When she was arrested, Perpetua and others in her group were still catechumens. Thus, while in jail they received an emergency baptism. Baptismal motifs would figure heavily in her visions.

Perpetua's father was a pagan who, after her arrest, begged her to do whatever the authorities asked. She refused, insisting she was a Christian. Her response infuriated him. Perpetua says, "My father was so angered by the word 'Christian' that he moved towards me as though he would pluck my eyes out."[110] We glimpse here the deep divisions that conversion to Christianity could cause within ancient families. An ancient pagan audience would have judged her behavior impious, profoundly disrespectful of one's elders. The charge of impiety was serious and a common one against early Christians, for converted Christians had to repudiate their family's gods and long-standing local and family traditions.[111] During her arraignment, Perpetua publicly confessed, "Yes, I am a Christian (*christiana sum*)."[112] That public confession was, technically speaking, the moment of her martyrdom. *Martyr*, after all, is the Greek word for "witness," and her admission was a public, life-defining witness of her faith. During her trial, I should add, the judge ordered her father beaten. Why? Because he had raised such a rebellious, such an impious daughter. In the judge's mind, Perpetua's father was an utter failure.[113]

Perpetua had an infant son. Prior to her trial, her father held up her baby and said, "Perform the sacrifice—have pity on your baby."[114] She refused, of course, but was able to bribe the guards, who allowed the baby to be brought in and stay with her in jail. She speaks in her diary about how much it comforted her to nurse her baby in jail.

She records in her brief memoir a series of remarkable dream-visions. Let me touch on just one of these. She sees a bronze ladder stretched from earth to heaven. Climbing seems perilous since the ladder is lined with swords, hooks, spikes, and daggers that could pierce the inattentive climber. Her catechist, Saturus, is already perched high on the ladder and calls to her to ascend, but she is frightened by a dragon that sits ominously at its base. In a dramatic moment, she calls on the name of Christ Jesus, steps on the dragon's head, and begins up the ladder. She suddenly finds herself standing in a vast garden among thousands wearing white robes. She comes up to a tall man with graying hair, dressed in shepherd's garb, milking sheep—clearly a Christ figure. He hands her a mouthful of milk, and the crowd says "Amen." She drinks it and it tastes sweet.[115]

All this plays on various threads of ancient North African baptismal catechesis and ritual. The ladder symbolizes Jesus' narrow way; the dragon is an Old Testament symbol of chaos and evil; Perpetua's stepping on its head alludes to the prophecy in Genesis in which a woman will crush the head of the tempter; the garden alludes to the commonplace teaching that baptism marks a return to the innocence of the Garden of Eden before the Fall; the white robes allude to clothing given the newly baptized after they come up naked from the water.

What about the milk? In the ancient world, immediately after baptism and chrismation, one witnessed the Eucharist for the first time and received one's first Communion. In some churches, one received at Communion not just one cup, but three. The first had water and was thought to give the newly baptized a sort of inner washing that paralleled the body's earlier outer washing. The third was the cup of consecrated wine, the Blood of Christ. Between these two was a cup of milk laced with honey. This symbolized, of course, that one is entering the Promised Land, the "land of milk and honey." In North Africa, the newly baptized were referred to as *infantes*, as "new-borns." Thus this drinking sweet-tasting milk symbolized spiritual baby food.[116]

Perpetua and her companions were sentenced to be executed. They were led into the amphitheatre in Carthage, and various wild animals were sent out to attack them. Perpetua's teacher, Saturus, was mauled by a leopard, and when his blood splattered the crowd, they mockingly cried, "Well washed! Well washed!" The author who witnessed this event believed the crowd's mocking held a deeper truth: that Perpetua and her companions were experiencing a baptism of blood, being washed in the blood of Christ. When the animals failed to attack Perpetua, the governor ordered a gladiator to execute her. The gladiator-executioner was apparently frightened; his hand trembled. She was unafraid and guided the sword to her throat.

The names of Perpetua and her companion, Felicity, were included among the famous saints listed in the Roman Canon, the ancient Eucharistic prayer of the Church of Rome. Her feast day was popular in North Africa. A series of sermons given by Saint Augustine celebrate her memory. I should add one bit of news: several Augustinian scholars have just announced a remarkable discovery of a long lost sermon by Augustine about Perpetua.[117]

3. Women as Authors: Proba

We know of only a few early Christian texts written by women. Perpetua's prison diary is perhaps the earliest. Another early text is a lengthy narrative poem (of nearly 700 lines) by Faltonia Betitia Proba (active, 360s). We know little about her except that she was from an upper-class Roman family, was married, and had several sons. Her husband served for a time as a provincial governor and later became the prefect of Rome.

Proba's poem belongs to a quite unusual genre known as a *cento*.[118] The Latin word *cento* literally means "patchwork." Think about making a quilt: one sews together scraps of old cloth to create this checkerboard patchwork, assembling something new and usable from discarded leftovers. That is what a *cento* does with words. The poet sews together a new poem by drawing together bits and scraps from someone else's earlier poems. Proba's *Cento* retells the biblical story concentrating mainly on stories from Genesis and the Gospels. The words are, technically speaking, not Proba's own. Every phrase is drawn from Vergil's poetry, mainly, the *Aeneid* and the *Ecologues*. This art form presumes real sophistication and the thorough command of an author. Imagine you had memorized the complete works of Shakespeare. From our vantage point, Shakespeare's English is a bit archaic and a bit arcane; we can understand it, of course, but that is hardly how we in the twenty-first century speak. Imagine that, using only Shakespeare's words, you retold the creation story from Genesis and the life of Jesus. That is the sort of thing Proba did with Vergil. In Proba's day, Vergil's Latin would have been about four centuries old. It was not the Latin of her time; it was venerable, classical Latin, a bit archaic and a bit arcane. Using Vergil, she wove a new Christian artwork from his old wording (not to mention, his distinctly pagan worldview). Here are the opening words:

> *Now, God almighty, accept my sacred.*
> *Song, I pray; unloose the utterance.*
> *Of your eternal, sevenfold Spirit, and so.*
> *Unlock the inmost sanctum of my heart.*
> *That I may find all mysteries within.*
> *My power to relate—I, Proba, prophetess .*
> *It is not my task, indeed, to publicize.*
> *My fame on the strength of words, thereby.*
> *To seek some small acclaim from human favor.*
> *But wet from the Castalian fount have I,*
> *In imitation of the blessed, and thirsting,*
> *Drunk the offerings of the holy day.*
> *And here shall I begin my song. Be present,*
> *God, make straight my power of mind!.*
> *That Virgil put to verse Christ's sacred duties let me tell.*[119]

In this prologue, Proba describes herself "wet" from the "font" (presumably because she was newly baptized) and "drunk" from the "offerings" (presumably because she deeply appreciates the power of the Eucharist). She speaks of herself as a prophetess, tasting inner mysteries and the Spirit's gifts. Her work is thus expressive of a vibrant spirituality of baptism.

4. Women as Pilgrims: Egeria

In 1884, scholars discovered a remarkable work written by another early Christian woman. It is an autobiographical work, a travelogue recording the experiences of a Spanish woman named Egeria (active, circa 400); it recounts her pilgrimage to the Holy Land and other sacred venues in the Middle East.[120] The surviving text is incomplete. Scholars' best guess is that we have the middle third of it. Egeria composed this account of her travels for the edification of a community of ascetic women she belonged to back in Spain. Given the care and hospitality she received everywhere she visited, it seems likely she was of some aristocratic background.

The very idea of making a pilgrimage to the Holy Land only emerges in the fourth century.[121] That the Holy Land, its geography, and sacred sites, looms so large in Christian consciousness owes much to such fourth-century pilgrims. In the 130s, in the wake of the Bar Kochba revolt, the Roman army completely leveled the already-devastated Jerusalem. Virtually nothing of the ancient Jewish city survived. Only decades later did imperial authorities allow the area to be resettled. Jerusalem, as fourth-century Christians knew it, was a strictly Roman city. Those fourth-century Christian pilgrims did not just visit the Holy Land. They brought back memories that ended up profoundly reshaping Western liturgies, notably those of Holy Week and Easter. Think, for instance, of the practice of the Stations of the Cross and of the veneration of the Cross on Good Friday. These pilgrims used to come back from the Holy Land to their home Church and say, "Now, bishop, that's not the way they do things in Jerusalem." The liturgies of Jerusalem, especially as they were developed under Cyril of Jerusalem and his successor, John, became a standard to be imitated and adopted by Churches around the Empire.

Egeria, in her *Itinerarium*, offers precious eyewitness accounts of several Jerusalem liturgies. Those of you familiar with the Rite of Christian Initiation of Adults know that on the first Sunday of Lent, we formally enroll catechumens for baptism, designating them as "elect," as "chosen ones" worthy for baptism. The earliest description we have of this ritual comes from Egeria. The Jerusalem rite, according to Egeria, had an air of high solemnity. During Lent, those who applied for baptism came with their sponsors to the main Church, the Martyrium, near where Jesus was believed to have been crucified. The bishop, seated on his *cathedra* in the center of the basilica and surrounded by a retinue of presbyters and deacons, questioned the godparent and neighbors of each candidate: "Does so-and-so lead a good life? Does he obey his parents? Is he a drunkard or a liar?" If the person was accepted, the bishop had the person's name formally enrolled for baptism; if denied, the bishop would say: "Let him amend his life, and when he has done so, let him then approach the baptismal font."[122]

Egeria also offers a valuable description of mystagogy. In the fourth century, the rites of Christian initiation—baptism, chrismation (what we now call confirmation), and Eucharist—were carefully guarded secrets. Only *after* initiation at the Easter Vigil did the newly baptized receive instruction about the rituals themselves. Before baptism, one had no idea what took place at the Eucharist. One would not have known how to receive Communion, let alone how Christians understood the Eucharist as the body and blood of Christ. These were "mysteries." That, by the way, is what the word *mystagogy* means, "the teaching of the mysteries." We have a number of mystagogical sermons from this era, sermons by Cyril of Jerusalem, John Chrysostom, Theodore of Mopsuestia, Ambrose, and Augustine.[123] Ancient preachers sometimes walked hearers step-by-step back through the rituals they experienced at Easter, explaining each act and its hidden meanings. What makes Egeria's account so helpful is the way she describes the setting and audience where all this took place. She says that in the eight days between Easter and its octave, the newly baptized would come together to hear the "mysteries." All unbaptized, whether catechumens or pagans, were barred from entering and listening. She says mystagogical sermons were given in the Anastasis, the Church of the Resurrection. She also noted the noisy enthusiasm and applause that greeted these talks: "While the bishop is discussing and explaining each point, so loud are the voices of praise that they can be heard outside the Church."[124]

Egeria visited other sacred locales. She recounts the rigors of climbing up Mount Sinai. She also visited the shrine of Saint Thecla in Seleucia, noting, "Having arrived there in the name of God, a prayer was given at the shrine and the complete *Acts of Saint Thecla* was read. I then gave unceasing thanks to Christ our God who granted to me, an unworthy woman and in no way deserving, the fulfillment of my desires in all things."[125]

5. Women as Monastic Founders: Macrina

The fourth century saw the sudden emergence of monasticism. While ascetical practices had been part and parcel of Christianity from the beginning, it is in the fourth century, after the legalization of Christianity, that asceticism assumes highly organized, institutional shape—what we now call monasticism. Women, we now recognize, played key roles in this development.[126] One was Macrina (circa 327–379), sometimes referred to as Macrina the Younger to distinguish her from her saintly grandmother, Macrina the Elder. Macrina was a member of one of the most remarkable families of early Christianity.

She grew up Cappadocia, a Roman province in what today is central Turkey. Her family was quite wealthy and owned land around Caesarea as well as up north in Pontus near the Black Sea. Her brothers, Basil of Caesarea (330–370) and Gregory of Nyssa (334–395), were two of the so-called

Cappadocian Fathers. Her brothers' names may be unfamiliar to you, but every Sunday we recite what we inaccurately refer to as the Nicene Creed but which comes, in fact, from the Cappadocian-led Council of Constantinople in 381.

The original creed of the Council of Nicaea (325) simply said "I believe in the Holy Spirit"—period—without any further phrases defining our belief in the Holy Spirit. In the intervening period between the two ecumenical councils, especially between 360 and 381, theologian-bishops debated the status of the Spirit: Is the Spirit truly God, truly one in being with the Father, as the Son is? Macrina's brothers, together with their good friend Gregory of Nazianzus, hammered out the classic defense of the divinity of the Holy Spirit. Of course, once you say Christ is God and the Holy Spirit is God, how do you not end up with three gods? So they also were the pathbreaking formulators of the doctrine of the Trinity. Gregory of Nyssa, in particular, would think these issues through with enormous sophistication.

It was Gregory who would write a memoir commemorating the life and wisdom of his sister, Macrina.[127] Macrina, like many women in those days, was betrothed at a very young age. The idea of choosing one's own mate is a thoroughly modern and Western phenomenon, only becoming commonplace in the nineteenth century. Marriage in the ancient world was not about romance or love. It was about raising a good, respectable family and enjoying a good, respectable social status. Ancient marriages were arranged by parents, often when their children were still children. Girls were engaged as young as eight and generally not older than thirteen or fourteen. Macrina was betrothed at age twelve to a fiancé who was twenty-five. Her fiancé died not long after, So to her family's surprise, she declared herself a widow, a virgin widow, and refused all efforts to get engaged to someone else.

Susanna Elm, in her pathbreaking study, *The Virgins of God*, has traced how Macrina slowly transformed her family first into an ascetical household and then into a monastic community. In the ancient world, there were strict and well-marked divisions between social classes, and there were certain household tasks that elite women, such as Macrina, simply should not do. One was housecleaning. We have all read those nineteenth-century British novels where the lines between the ruling class and the servants who clean the house or work the kitchen are strictly drawn. Macrina broke down class barriers, initially the simple ones like doing servants' tasks. Later she had the family's household slaves freed, and then took things a great leap further. As Gregory put it, she "persuaded her [mother] to place herself on the same level as the group of virgins to share with them one table, one lodging, and all the necessities of life, like an equal, all differences of rank having been removed from their lives."[128]

It is hard for us Americans, accustomed to our longstanding tradition of social equality, to savor how revolutionary this shattering of social barriers is. But Macrina was convinced that this is what Christian life was all about: recognizing the sacred and equal dignity of every person. Years later she and her household took in groups of women refugees who wandered the nearby roads during a time of famine. Initially she gave them aid and hospitality. Eventually they too became members of Macrina's ascetic household. And so Macrina slowly formed what we would now call a monastic community, with herself as a sort of abbess.

Macrina's brother, Basil of Caesarea, is regarded in the Greek East the way Saint Benedict is regarded in the Latin West; namely, as the great legislator of Christian monasticism. It is now clear that Basil drew some of his inspiration from his sister's experiments in monastic life. I should add that Gregory of Nyssa authored not only a *Life of Saint Macrina*, but also composed a brilliant dialogue entitled *On the Soul and the Resurrection*.[129] In it, he sets out what the dying Macrina taught him about the Christian understanding of the resurrection while on her deathbed. Educated ancients would have spotted immediately Gregory's quite self-conscious literary parallel: Macrina handed on her wisdom about death and dying and resurrection on her deathbed much as Socrates (in Plato's *Apology*) taught his disciples about death and dying and true wisdom on his deathbed. Gregory portrayed her, in other words, as a philosopher—a "lover of wisdom" in the literal sense of the word. Only her philosophy was Christianity, and Christianity taught this outrageous new doctrine: resurrection.

6. Women as Intellectuals & Patrons: Melania the Elder

Another extraordinary early Christian woman was Melania the Elder (342–411).[130] I think of Melania as a sort of Jackie Kennedy of the ancient world. She was one of the wealthiest women in the Roman Empire. She was married, at a young age, to the prefect of the city of Rome. She also suffered much tragedy. There were miscarriages. She became a widow at age twenty-two. With all that money at stake, her relatives put enormous pressure on her to remarry. She refused.

In 374, she packed up all the wealth she could carry, put it on a ship, and sailed off to Alexandria. She wanted to see monks. Monasticism, as I mentioned, was one of those remarkable enterprises that springs up in the fourth century. She would have first heard of monks as a young girl growing up in Rome. She may have seen those black-robed men who accompanied Saint Athanasius of Alexandria during his exile in Rome in the 340s. In the late 350s, Athanasius' *Life of Antony*, the brilliant biography of one of monasticism's pioneers, was translated into Latin and circulated in sophisticated circles in Rome. Now a young woman, she wanted to see monks firsthand.

Greeted as a celebrity upon her arrival in Alexandria, she was led by the venerable Isidore the Hosteller out to the desert to Nitria, a city of monks perched on the edge of the sprawling Libyan Desert. There she met one of its leaders, Abba Pambo. Melania decided to give the monks of Nitria a taste of her munificence, donating a large coffer loaded with silver. When Melania announced her donation, Pambo simply sat there, weaving rope out of palm leaves. He hardly looked up from his work, but gave her a brief, perfunctory blessing and directed his assistant to distribute the silver throughout the monasteries of Egypt. Melania was miffed. In a world where patrons enjoyed effusive praise, she deserved more. So she spoke up. "You should know, sir, how much it is: there are 300 pounds." He then said, "My child, the One who measures mountains knows the amount of silver. If you were giving it to me, you spoke well. But if you were giving it to God…, then be quiet." As Melania told her biographer years later, "Thus did the Lord show his power."[131]

She eventually settled in the Holy Land and built a double monastery on the Mount of Olives just outside of Jerusalem. She led the women's community, while her friend and co-worker, Rufinus of Aquileia (345–410), led the men's side. The two would create one of the foremost intellectual centers of early Christianity, a sort of monastic think tank. Rufinus would achieve fame—and notoriety— for his many translations into Latin of Greek theological and monastic works. Over the next thousand years, when the whole Latin Middle Ages forgot how to read Greek, Rufinus's translations became the mainstay of what medievals depended on for their knowledge of the Greek theological tradition as well as their recollection of early Church history. Melania was herself a remarkable intellectual. While Latin was her native language, she was fluent in Greek and capable of doing what Latin intellectuals such as Saint Augustine could not: read Greek theological works, such as Origen's voluminous works, in the original Greek.

Melania attracted other intellectuals. She converted one of Gregory of Nazianzus' disciples, the deacon Evagrius Ponticus (345–399), to the monastic life and sent him on to her friends in Egypt.[132] There Evagrius emerged as a pioneer of Christian mysticism and as the first great Christian psychologist, best known for his theory of the seven deadly sins.

Another of the intellectuals in Melania's circle was Palladius of Helenopolis, who wrote the first biography of John Chrysostom and also authored the *Lausiac History*, a compendium of brief biographies of holy people he met in Egypt and elsewhere. Palladius is one of our key sources for the life of Melania.

Melania was not only an intellectual. She was most important as a patron, a benefactor who financed both Christian monasticism and Christian scholarship. Unfortunately, Saint Jerome came to detest Rufinus, an old friend of his from school. During the Origenist controversy (390s–410s), Jerome used his enormous talents as a writer, polemicist, and satirist to blacken Rufinus's theological and personal reputation; Jerome also used his pen to blacken Melania's reputation—which is the reason she is not *Saint* Melania the Elder.

7. Women as Deaconesses: Olympias of Constantinople

Melania exemplifies a key role that women played in the early Church: benefactor. Another exemplar of this ministry was Saint Olympias of Constantinople (361–408). What we know of her comes from two major sources: an anonymous *Life of Saint Olympias* and her correspondence with the saintly and controversial bishop-preacher, John Chrysostom. Olympias was the daughter of a high-ranking courtier in Constantinople, capital of the Roman Empire. At age twenty-three, she married a much older man who died just two years later. At age thirty, she was ordained a deaconess by Nectarius, then bishop of Constantinople.

What is a deaconess? The office is well described in one of the most important liturgical documents of the early Church, the so-called *Apostolic Constitutions*. Here is the passage that defines the role of deaconess:

> *Ordain also a deaconess, faithful and holy, for the services pertaining to women, for whenever the bishop cannot send a male deacon to certain women's households because of the unbelievers, you shall thus send a woman deaconess, because of the suspicions of wicked people. For we require a woman as deaconess for many needs. First of all, in the baptism of women, the deacon shall anoint only their foreheads with holy oil and after him the deaconess shall anoint them, for there is no need for women to be observed by men.*[133]

Note the final sentence: During the baptismal rite, deaconesses anointed the women. In early Christianity, baptism was done in the nude, and the baptismal anointing was a full-body anointing. That, as the document notes, was one obvious reason deaconesses were needed.

The word *deacon* is from the Greek *diakonos*, which means "servant," "slave." Deacons and deaconesses handled what we would call social ministry. Olympias as a deaconess committed her enormous wealth, as well as her time and energy, to serving the needs of the poor of Constantinople. She, like Melania, also served as superior (*hēgoumenē*) of a large monastic community (its membership numbered at least 250). She also, like Melania, was a friend of leading Christian intellectuals. One of her friends was Gregory of Nyssa, who pioneered Christian Trinitarian theology and celebrated the life and wisdom of his sister Macrina. Another was the brilliantly eloquent bishop of Constantinople, John Chrysostom. When Chrysostom's political and ecclesiastical enemies got him sent into exile, Olympias supported him and helped keep him alive. There survives a remarkable and touching correspondence between the two.[134]

8. Women as Ascetics: Syncletica

It is popular nowadays to speak of "desert mothers" as though there was a movement of female hermits living in the Egyptian deserts that mirrored and matched the vibrant colonies of male anchorites then earning fame around the Roman Empire. Desert monasticism is a longstanding area of my research, and I have not found good evidence for desert mothers, at least in any literal sense of the term. I realize, of course, that in the famous sixth-century anthology *Sayings of the Fathers* (*Apophthegmata Patrum*), there are three women numbered as *ammas* ("mothers") mixed in with its 120 *abbas* ("fathers").[135] These women did not live in the desert: one lived in the suburbs of Alexandria and a second in the Nile Delta.

The search for desert mothers misses where the real action was. The real action was in and around prosperous and populous towns up and down the Nile River, where Christian women gathered to create small ascetic households not unlike those Macrina had created in Pontus.[136] In Egypt, there also emerged these large and highly organized monastic communities of women that paralleled certain large and highly organized monastic communities of men. One famous double monastery was headed by Pachomius (died 346), an early organizer of Christian monasticism; another was headed by Shenoute of Atripe (died circa 464), a flamboyant and highly articulate leader of Coptic monasticism. Recent studies have highlighted that while these men had official oversight, women superiors often exercised remarkable independence and could be real forces to be reckoned with.[137] But these women-monks were not desert mothers located in the arid wastes; their monasteries were within the confines of the verdant Nile valley. We only get passing glimpses of their lives. Surviving sources on Egyptian monasticism devote little narrative space to women, their organizations, their spiritual development, and their monastic theology. There is no Egyptian equivalent to Gregory of Nyssa's *Life of Macrina* that might allow us to trace the progress of women's asceticism at closer range. Women's asceticism in Egypt is underreported. The evidence, while faint and fragmentary, implies that women's asceticism had sizable numbers, varied lifestyles, and considerable vigor.

One of those Egyptian women ascetics celebrated in the *Sayings of the Fathers*, Amma Syncletica (active, early fifth century).[138] She lived on the outskirts of one of the great cities of the ancient world, Alexandria, at the mouth of the Nile. She would have seen firsthand its beautiful harbors and its famous lighthouse. In one of her sayings, she draws on a most undesertlike image—a sailing image—to articulate her spirituality: "When we are driven by spirits who are against us; we hold to the cross of Christ as our sail so we can set a safe course."[139]

Conclusion

This seems a good note to close on. The women we have seen here sailed on often tempestuous cultural seas and survived, even flourished, in those storms by holding fast to the cross of Christ. Their bravado may provide some encouragement for women today who may find the seas only slightly less choppy.

NOTES

95. Several excellent anthologies have compiled and translated these sources: Mary R. Lefkowitz and Maureen B. Fant, ed. and trans. *Women's Life in Greece & Rome: A Sourcebook in Translation*, 2nd ed. (Baltimore: Johns Hopkins Press, 1992); Ross Shepherd Kraemer, ed., *Women's Religions in the Greco-Roman World: A Sourcebook* (New York: Oxford University Press, 2004); and Patricia Cox Miller, ed., *Women in Early Christianity: Translations from Greek Texts* (Washington: Catholic University of America Press, 2005). For a valuable introduction to the social world of early Christian women, see especially Gillian Clark, *Women in Late Antiquity: Pagan and Christian Lifestyles* (New York: Oxford University Press, 1994).

96. Epigraph from second-century Pergamum; cited in Lefkowitz and Fant, 265.

97. Jerome, *Against Helvidius* 20; trans. Elizabeth A. Clark, *Women in the Early Church*, Message of the Fathers, vol. 13 (Collegeville: The Liturgical Press, 1984), 99.

98. *Inscriptiones Latinae Selectae* (ca. 2nd cent.), no. 9980, 9927, 9497, 9683, 33892; trans. Lefkowitz and Fant, 222-224.

99. John Chrysostom, *De sacerdotio* [*On the Priesthood*] 1; trans. Graham Neville, *Saint John Chrysostom: On the Priesthood* (Crestwood, NY: St. Vladimir's Seminary Press, 1977), 38-39.

100. *Oxyrhynchus papyrus*, no. 744 (ca. 1B.C.E.); trans. Lefkowitz and Fant, 187.

101. Galen, *De usu partium* [*On the Use of the Parts of the Body*], 14.6-7; trans. Lefkowitz and Fant, 244-245.

102. Clark, *Women in Late Antiquity*, vii.

103. For a translation, see Bart A. Ehrman, *After the New Testament: A Reader in Early Christianity* (New York: Oxford University Press, 1998). For a helpful study, see Susan A. Calef, "Thecla 'Tried and True' and the Inversion of Romance," in *A Feminist Companion to the New Testament Apocrypha*, ed. Amy-Jill Levine (London: T&T Clark, 2006), 163-185.

104. *Acts of Paul and Thecla* 5-6; trans. Ehrman, 279. For an illuminating study of celibacy, its history, variety, and development, see Peter Brown, *The Body and Society: Men, Women, and Sexual Renunciation in Early Christianity* (New York: Columbia University Press, 1988).

105. *Acts of Paul and Thecla* 34-35.

106. Tertullian, *De baptismo* [*On Baptism*] 17; trans. E.A. Clark, 173.

107. See Stephen J. Davis, *Cult of St. Thecla*, Oxford Early Christian Studies (New York: Oxford University Press, 2001).

108. Now in the Louvre in Paris; see http://commons.wikimedia.org/wiki/Image:Ampoule_Thècle_01.JPG .

109. For the text with a parallel English translation, see Herbert Murusillo, ed., *The Acts of the Christian Martyrs* (Oxford: Clarendon, 1972), 101-131. For an analysis, see Joyce E. Salisbury, *Perpetua's Passion: The Death and Memory of a Young Roman Woman* (New York: Routledge, 1998). See also the classic survey by W.H.C. Frend, *Martyrdom and Persecution in the Early Church: A Study of a Conflict from the Maccabees to Donatus* (Oxford: Blackwell, 1965).

110. *Passio s. Perpetuae* 3; trans. Murusillo, 109.

111. On this important issue, see Robert L. Wilken, *Christians as the Romans Saw Them*, 2nd ed. (New Haven: Yale University Press, 2003).

112. *Passio s. Perpetuae* 6; trans. Harmless.

113. *Passio s. Perpetuae* 6; trans. Murusillo, 113-115. See Frend, *Martyrdom*, 322.

114. *Passio s. Perpetuae* 6; trans. Murusillo, 113.

115. *Passio s. Perpetuae* 4; trans. Murusillo, 111.

116. The three cups are mentioned in *Apostolic Tradition* 21, attributed to Hippolytus. On this ancient and influential account of the baptismal rite, see Paul Bradshaw, Maxwell E. Johnson, & L. Edward Phillips, ed., *The Apostolic Tradition: A Commentary*, Hermeneia Series (Minneapolis, MN: Fortress Press, 2002).

117. Augustine, *Sermones* 280-282. In May 2008 it was announced that six new sermons of Augustine have just been discovered by I. Schiller, D. Weber und C. Weidmann in a twelfth-century manuscript in the Bibliotheca Amploniana in Erfurt, Germany. *Sermo Erfurt 1* (as they are now calling it) was delivered on the feast of St. Perpetua.

118. For the text and a translation of Proba's *Cento*, see Elizabeth A. Clark & Diane F. Hatch, ed., *The Golden Bough, The Oaken Cross: The Virgilian Cento of Faltonia Betitia Proba* (Chico, CA: Scholars Press, 1981). For an analysis, see Elizabeth A. Clark, "Faltonia Betitia Proba and Her Virgilian Poem: The Christian Matron as Artist," in *Ascetic Piety and Women's Faith: Essays on Late Ancient Christianity*, Studies in Women and Religion 20 (Lewiston: Edwin Mellen Press, 1986), 124-152.

119. Proba, *Cento* ll. 1-23; trans. E. Clark, *Ascetic*, 155-156.

120. For the translation, see George Gingras, trans., *Egeria: Diary of a Pilgrimage*, Ancient Christian Writers, vol. 38 (New York: Newman Press, 1970). For a study, see John Wilkinson, *Egeria's Travels* (reprint: Aris & Phillips, 1999).

121. On this new phenomenon of pilgrimage, E.D. Hunt, *Holy Land Pilgrimage in the Later Roman Empire, A.D. 312-460* (Oxford: Clarendon Press, 1982); Robert L. Wilken, *The Land Called Holy: Palestine in Christian History and Thought* (New Haven: Yale University Press, 1992).

122. Egeria, *Itinerarium* 45; trans. Gingras, 122.

123. On this, see William Harmless, *Augustine and the Catechumenate* (Collegeville, MN: Liturgical Press, 1995).

124. Egeria, *Itinerarium* 47; trans. Gingras, 125.

125. Egeria, *Itinerarium* 23; trans. Gingras, 87.

126. On the emergence of monasticism, see William Harmless, *Desert Christians: An Introduction to the Literature of Early Monasticism* (New York: Oxford University Press, 2004); on recent scholarly trends, see William Harmless, "Monasticism," in *The Oxford Handbook of Early Christian Studies*, ed. Susan Ashbrook Harvey and David Hunter (New York: Oxford University Press, 2008), 493-517.

127. For a translation of Gregory's *Life of Macrina*, see Joan M. Petersen, ed., *Handmaids of the Lord: Contemporary Descriptions of Feminine Asceticism in the First Six Christian Centuries*, Cistercian Publications 143 (Kalamazoo, MI: Cistercian Publications, 1996). For an excellent study, see Susanna Elm, *Virgins of God: The Making of Asceticism in Late Antiquity*, Oxford Classical Monographs (New York: Oxford University Press, 1994), 25-105.

128. Gregory of Nyssa, *Vita. s. Macrinae* 11; trans. Elm, 84.

129. Gregory of Nyssa, *On the Soul and the Resurrection*, trans. Catharine P. Roth (Crestwood, NY: St. Vladimir's Seminary Press, 1993). For a study, see Rowan Williams, "Macrina's Deathbed Revisited: Gregory of Nyssa on Mind and Passion," in L. Wickham and C. Bammel, *Christian Faith and Greek Philosophy in Late Antiquity*, Supplement to Vigiliae Christianae 19 (Leiden: Brill, 1993).

130. Our major ancient source on Melania is the brief account of her life by her friend, Palladius of Helenopolis. For a translation, see Robert T. Meyer, ed., *Palladius: The Lausiac History*, Ancient Christian Writers 34 (New York: Paulist Press, 1965). On Melania, see Harmless, *Desert Christians*, 1-2.

131. Palladius, *Historia Lausiaca* 10; trans. Meyer, 44-45.

132. On Evagrius, see Harmless, *Desert Christians*, 311-367; and Luke Dysinger, *Psalmody and Prayer in the Writings of Evagrius Ponticus*, Oxford Theological Monographs (New York: Oxford University Press, 2005).

133. *Apostolic Constitutions* III.16; trans. E. Clark, *Women in the Early Church*, 180-181. For an overview of the role of the deaconess, see Elm, *Virgins of God*, 137-183.

134. Elm, *Virgins*, 181, speaks, with justice, of John as Olympias' "soul-mate." For the correspondence, see A.M. Malingrey, ed., *Jean Chrysostome: Lettres à Olympias; Vie anonyme d'Olympias*, Sources chrétiennes 13bis (Paris: Cerf, 1968).

135. For a translation, see Benedicta Ward, trans., *Sayings of the Desert Fathers: The Alphabetical Collection*, Cistercian Studies 59 (Kalamazoo: Cistercian Publications, 1984). For a discussion of this issue of "desert mothers," see Harmless, *Desert Christians*, 440-445.

136. There are intriguing reports in the fifth-century *History of the Monks in Egypt* (see Harmless, *Desert Christians*, chapter 9); also chance findings, such as a papyrus (*P. Oxy.* 3203) that preserves a rental contract between a Jewish man and two women described as *monachai apotaktikai*, "female-monk renouncers" (Harmless, *Desert Christians*, 25).

137. On this, see Rebecca Krawiec, *Shenoute and the Women of the White Monastery: Egyptian Monasticism in Late Antiquity* (New York: Oxford University Press, 2002).

138. The source for these sayings is a fifth-century work, *The Life and Regimen of the Holy and Blessed Teacher Syncletica*, wrongly attributed to Athanasius (who would have been long dead). The work opens with a brief biography, then presents her ascetical teaching (much indebted to Evagrius). For a translation, see Elizabeth Bryson Bongie, *The Life of Blessed Syncletica by Pseudo-Athanasius* (Toronto: Peregrina Publishing, 1996). For a study, see A.S.E. Parker, "The Vita Syncleticae: Its Manuscripts, Ascetical Teachings and Its Use in Monastic Sources," *Studia Patristica* 30 (1997): 231-234.

139. *Apophthegmata Patrum* [*Sayings of the Fathers*] Syncletica 9; trans. Ward, 232-233.

4. Women of the Middle Ages

Gary Macy, PhD, The John Nobili, SJ, Professor of Theology
Santa Clara University

In the Middle Ages, women played a far larger role in the life of the Church than they would in later centuries. In the early Middle Ages, they performed both sacramental and administrative functions that would be reserved for men after the thirteenth century. They celebrated the Mass, distributed Communion, read the Gospel, heard confessions, and preached. Some abbesses also exercised episcopal power, and a few were considered bishops. The powerful Abbess of Las Huelgas in Spain continued to wear her miter and exercise administrative episcopal power until 1874. This paper will discuss the evidence for these claims.

Celebration of the Eucharist

Evidence from the fourth through the eleventh centuries indicates that a few women led liturgies with the approval of at least some bishops. The scarcity of evidence does not necessarily mean that the practice was unusual, however. The sources that do survive, of necessity, have been compiled by an elite, almost exclusively male intelligentsia. They wrote the documents and preserved them. Universities, monasteries, convents, dioceses, and the Roman curia had the means and motive to preserve particular records, and modern scholars of necessity rely heavily upon them. Because of this clear bias, the picture presented here cannot be and will not be complete. In fact, given that writers from the thirteenth century on assumed women could never have led the liturgy, it is amazing how much evidence has survived.

A graffito dated between fourth and sixth century and found near Poitiers commemorates that "Martia the presbytera made the offering together with Olybrius and Nepos." [140] Scholars who have studied the carving agree that this inscription refers to Martia as a minister who celebrated the Eucharist along with two men, Olybrius and Nepos.[141] The Council of Nîmes, held in 394, noting that "women seemed to have been assumed into levitical service," ordered that "such ordination should be undone when it is effected contrary to reason. It should be seen that no one so presume in the future."[142] It is quite likely that the ministry of women to the Eucharist was being discussed here, although some scholars have argued it was the deaconate rather than the presbyterate that the Council intended to forbid.[143] Ninety years later, in his 494 letter to the bishops of southern Italy and Sicily, Pope Gelasius also spoke out against bishops who were allowing women to serve at the altar. Gelasius had heard that "women are confirmed to minister at the sacred altars and to perform all matters imputed only to the service of the male sex and for which women are not competent."[144] The Italian scholar Giorgio Otranto makes clear in his analysis of this letter that Gelasius was directing his ire at bishops who were ordaining women to function as priests, not at the women themselves.[145]

Fifteen years later, Bishops Licinius, Melanius, and Eustochius of northern Gaul wrote to two priests from Brittany. They were furious to learn that the priests traveled with women who assisted them at the altar "so that, while you are distributing the Eucharist, they hold the chalices and presume to administer the blood of Christ to the people of God."[146] The women were referred to by their companions as *conhospitae* ("housemates"), indicating that the women were living with the priests if indeed they were not their wives. The bishops upbraided the priests for "this novelty and unheard-of superstition" that "brings infamy upon the clergy and…incurs shame and horror for the holy religion." The bishops demanded that "silly little women (*mulierculae*) of this sort not pollute the holy sacraments by illicit assistance," and forbade the priests to continue to live in the same house with them.[147] On the other hand, the letter implied that at least these priests and their congregations accepted the women as co-ministers of the Eucharist.

In his 747 reply to Frankish authorities who wished to know if nuns could read the Gospel or sing at Mass, Pope Zachary said no, adding, "Nevertheless, as we have heard to our dismay, divine worship has fallen into such disdain that women have presumed to serve at the sacred altars, and that the female sex, to whom it does not belong, perform all the things that are assigned exclusively to men."[148] Women, it would seem, were still ministering at the altar in the mid-eighth century. At the 829 Council of Paris, the bishops were appalled to learn that "in some provinces, in contradiction to the divine law and to canonical instruction, women betake themselves into the altar area and impudently take hold of the sacred vessels, hold out the priestly garments to the priest, and—what is still worse, more indecent and unfitting than all this—they give the people the body and blood of the Lord and do other things which in themselves are indecent."[149] As in the sixth century, it appears that at least some priests and bishops were allowing women to minister at the altar. Perhaps they were participating as deaconesses or perhaps as priests. This depends on whether the "things which it would be shameful to mention" referred to saying the Mass itself. A report to the bishops of the acts of the council from the same year makes it clear that some bishops had been allowing the practice: "doubtless it occurred through the carelessness and negligence of some bishops…[they] have given themselves to carnal passions and illicit actions, so that women, without anyone preventing them, betake themselves into consecrated houses and therein have been able to introduce unpermitted things."[150]

The reference to the bishops' "carnal passions" might indicate as well that these bishops were married, and so the slur against the bishops that it was only lust that forced the clergy to allow the women to serve at the altar has to be taken with a grain of salt. It is important to remember here that deacons, priests, and bishops were married in the Western as well as the Eastern Church until celibacy was enforced by in the mid-twelfth century. The wives of priests and deacons were sometimes called female priests (*presbyterae*) and deaconesses (*diacona, diaconissa*) in contemporary literature. In this case, the sources might be speaking of married *presbyterae* or deaconesses who shared in the liturgy with their spouses.

Women certainly did distribute Communion in the tenth, eleventh, and perhaps twelfth centuries. Texts for these services, with prayers written with feminine word endings, exist in two manuscripts of this period.[151] One was copied in the eleventh or twelfth century at the Abbey of Saint Sophia in Benevento for use by the nuns in that community.[152] The second dates from the tenth or eleventh century and, while the provenance of the manuscript is unknown, the use of the feminine word endings leads scholars to believe it too was used by nuns.[153] The famous medieval scholar and Benedictine monk Jean Leclerq notes, "It is never said or supposed that the one who recites [these prayers] is a priest. Nevertheless, in their ensemble they really constitute a long eucharistic prayer."[154] The rite consists of a series of prayers followed by a Communion service and prayers after Communion. Again, according to Leclerq: "Note that this ensemble [which makes up the opening prayers] corresponds more or less to the series of texts which serve as an introduction to the Mass: entrance psalm, litany, penitential rite, collect, and profession of faith."[155]

While these rites for women do not seem to be Masses, they are very close to them and indicate that women were still involved in service at the altar despite the many injunctions against them doing so. Further, since the books that preserve these rites are liturgical books we can presume, again to quote Leclerq, that "one did not incur the expense of copying manuscripts which would not be used; thus we have every reason to suppose that they were used, and in more than one place."[156] Once again, these prayers demonstrate that the practice of women serving at the altar persisted long after legislation had forbidden it, in fact, at least until the twelfth century.

One example of just such a Communion service was mentioned by the ninth-century hagiographer of Saint Odilia. The holy woman died while her sisters were in prayer. Alarmed that she had died without receiving the body and blood of Christ, they prayed that her soul return to her body. The miracle was granted (although Odilia was annoyed about it). "And when the chalice in which the Lord's body and blood were contained was ordered to be brought to her, accepting it with her own hands, and participating in the holy Communion, she handed over her soul while all watched."[157] The hagiographer seems to have had no problem with nuns handling the consecrated species, with Saint Odilia touching the chalice, and with nuns performing their own Communion rites.

Hearing Confessions

The main duty of an abbess was very similar to that of an abbot. Abbots and abbesses were quite powerful, sometimes as powerful as bishops, as we shall see later. Given their high standing in the Christian community, it is not too surprising that throughout this period abbesses exercised functions later reserved to the male diaconate and presbyterate.

The best example would be the responsibility, indeed duty, of the abbess to hear her nuns' confessions.[158] This practice is mentioned by at least two of the rules for nuns from the early medieval period. The writers go on at great length about the necessity of the abbess (or her designate) to hear daily confessions.[159] One of the main virtues required of an abbess was a merciful yet firm use of penance to train the nuns under her care. Abbesses heard their nuns' confessions, gave them penances, and reconciled them back into the community. There is no provision in either monastic rules or canonical legislation for nuns to confess to anyone other than their abbess or her delegate. For all intents and purposes, abbesses played the same role for their communities in hearing confession and in absolving from sin as bishops or priests did for their own communities. The abbesses' power to remove nuns from either table or the divine office or both is regularly termed excommunication and parallels within the community of nuns the power of bishops to excommunicate within the larger community of the Church.[160]

Abbesses sometimes even heard the confessions of and gave penances for people other than the nuns of their immediate communities. According to her hagiographer, Saint Bertila heard confessions for the entire surrounding area. "[Bertila] drew the family of the monastery or the surrounding neighbors through holy Communion, so that, hearing their confessions, they would do penance for their sins."[161] The "family of the monastery" would include, in this case, all those who worked in and for the monastery, including the peasant farmers in villages owned by the monastery. Saint Ite heard the confession and gave penance to a murderer who sought her out to hear his confession. When he refused to complete his penance, she had to give him another penance that he finally fulfilled.[162]

Abbesses then for several centuries were recognized as the ordinary ministers of penance for their own monastic communities and sometimes even exercised that power outside that circle. This was one of the most important liturgical functions attached to the *ordo* of abbess. Abbesses also exercised other functions later reserved for male clergy, particularly in their role as acting bishops for the territories under the jurisdiction of their convents. Before looking at this important history, however, it would help to review the data we have on women as bishops, whether abbesses or not.

Female Bishops and Abbesses As Bishops

Only five known references to women bishops exist in Western Christianity. By far the most famous is the ninth-century mosaic of *Theodora episcopa* in the Chapel of Saint Zeno in the Church of Santa Pressede in Rome. An inscription on a reliquary in the same Church that identifies Theodora as the mother of Pope Paschal I (817–824) dates the translation of the relics contained therein to July 20, 817. The *Liber pontificalis* named the father of Pascal I as Bonosus without further title. More than likely, if Bonosus had clerical status, this would have been noted, so it is unlikely that Theodora was the wife of a bishop.[163]

The other epigraphic inscription offers less information. A tomb dating sometime between the fourth and sixth centuries is inscribed to the "venerable woman, *episcopa* Q." Ute Eisen has identified the inscription as originally from Umbria and points out that there are also inscriptions to *presbyterae* from the same period and location that may indicate a pattern of female leadership in fifth-century Umbria.[164] Madigan and Osiek locate the inscription in Rome and suggest a date of 390. They also offer a tentative identification of "Q" as that of the mother or wife of Pope Siricius (384–399).[165]

Brigid of Ireland was described not only as a bishop, but also as having successfully undergone consecration to the ranks of the episcopacy. The ninth-century Celtic life of Brigid, the *Bethu Brigte*, described how it happened. "The bishop being intoxicated with the grace of God there did not recognize what he was reciting from his book, for he consecrated Brigid with the orders of a bishop. 'This virgin alone in Ireland,' said Mel, 'will hold the episcopal ordination.' While she was being consecrated a fiery column ascended from her head."[166] The reference is extraordinary for several reasons. First, Brigid was described as actually ordained to the episcopacy. She was not referred to as a bishop out of courtesy or metaphorically. She was actually ordained, even if by accident and even if uniquely. Second, there is no question that the ordination took. As Bishop Mel realized, once consecrated, Brigid was a bishop. At least for this ninth-century Irish writer, a woman could be ordained, even as bishop.

The second reference to the consecration of a woman as a bishop occurs on the tombstone of Mathilda, daughter of Otto I, who died in 968. Here she is described not only as abbess but also as *metropolitana* of Quedlinburg. *Metropolitanus* is a title most commonly used for an archbishop, although it very occasionally appears as the title for an abbot who acts as an archbishop. In this case, Mathilda was described an abbess who was considered as least in her epigraph as having episcopal authority.[167]

Hildeburga, the wife of Segenfrid, bishop of Le Mans from 963–996, was described as an *episcopissa* in the account of Segenfrid's death. The bishop was remembered disparagingly in the mid-eleventh century continuation of the *Acts of the Bishops of Le Mans* because he married and because he bequeathed a large portion of the Church's property to his son. Churches were treated as hereditary during this period, so it is difficult to know if Segenfrid really abused Church property or whether the author simply disapproved in general of married clergy. In this particular instance, the title of bishop was certainly given to Hildeburga because she was the wife of a male bishop. This does not mean, however, that she had no other function. Those of us who are married realize that simply being a husband or a wife does not exhaust one's vocation.

The earliest evidence that abbesses were considered the equivalent of bishops comes from the earliest existent rite for the ordination of an abbess. A group of manuscripts dating from the eighth to the fourteenth centuries preserves the rites of the Mozarabic or Visigoth Church of Spain. These rites would have been practiced from the fifth century roughly through the eleventh century for many parts of Christian Spain and in the diocese of Toledo up to the present day. The critical edition of the oldest manuscript, however, would represent rites from roughly the seventh through eleventh centuries.

The rite, which is clearly marked as the *ordination* of an abbess, begins,

When an abbess dedicated to God is ordained, she is clothed in the sanctuary with religious vestments and the religious mitre is placed upon her head and, with other women devoted to God preceding and following her with candles, she comes to the choir. The bishop then leads her to the altar; together with her, he places the pallium over her head, and says over her the following prayer:

Almighty Lord God before whom there is no distinction between the sexes, nor any difference between holy souls; you who strengthen men for the spiritual struggle, in order that you do not abandon women, we yield to your compassion in humble supplication, in order that this strengthened woman might acquire your mercy and this aided woman might not yield, whom by imposition of our hands and by the covering of this veil we desire to become mother to this holy flock of virgins. Give her, Lord, strength to wage spiritual war, as you bestowed provisions on the warrior Deborah, battle-ready for the struggle against the enemy troops of Sisera.[168]

The prayer continues in a similar warlike vein. The ceremony ends with the bishop kissing the new abbess and handing her a book of the rule (presumably the Rule of Benedict) and a staff.

Several points are worth noting here. First, the abbess receives a mitre, a pallium, and a staff. The mitre was most often used by bishops, even during this period, and so this is clearly a sign of administrative authority. The word *pallium* is more problematic. Tempting as it is to read *pallium* here as the vestment with the same name sent by the pope to a new bishop, this pallium is almost certainly a veil. The word referred to the veil received by a widow by the tenth council of Toledo in 656 and contemporary French and Irish references use the term to refer to the veil of a nun.[169] This is even more likely the meaning because the pallium is placed on the head of the one to be ordained, and the abbess is described as veiled in the prayer of ordination.

Still, the reference is significant, since veiling was an important part of the ordination rite of deaconesses as preserved in the tenth century Romano-Germanic Pontifical. Abbesses were often understood to be the successors to the order of deaconesses by writers in the tenth through twelfth centuries. The identification of abbesses and deaconesses, according to these sources, explained why abbesses had the authority to read the Gospel. A staff was a common symbol of office for bishops, abbots, and abbesses during this period and so is not unusual except that, insofar as the three ministries share this symbol of office, it would also suggest that they had shared responsibilities.

In the ordination rights for abbots in the Mozarabic rite, neither the mitre nor the pallium are bestowed.[170] It is not surprising, of course, that an abbot does not receive the pallium if indeed a veil is meant, but it is very interesting that he does not receive the mitre, as does an abbess. This may possibly suggest that abbesses had more administrative authority in Spain than did abbots.

One abbess in Spain, the powerful Cistercian abbess of Las Huelgas near Burgos, clearly acted as a bishop. She wore her mitre and carried her crosier until she was finally forbidden to do so in 1873. The history of Las Huelgas is impressive. Alphonsus VIII of Castile and his wife, Elinor of England (daughter of the more famous Elinor of Aquitaine), decided to establish the monastery of Las Huelgas after Alphonsus' victory over the Moslem armies at Cuenca in 1178. Pope Clement II approved the foundation in January of 1187, and the founding privilege was promulgated by the king in June of that year. From the very beginning, the monastery comprised noblewomen and was intended as the burial place for the royal family.

One of the first nuns was the king's daughter Constanza. In 1189, Las Huelgas was established as the motherhouse for all the Cistercian nuns in Castile and Leon, even though some of the Cistercian convents in those regions predated the establishment of Las Huelgas. In 1212, Alphonsus appointed the Abbess of Las Huelgas as administratrix and superior of the Hospital del Rey, a pilgrim lodge and poorhouse to which were attached a number of villages and villas. The hospital itself was staffed by a military order, the *Freyles*, and when the Abbess took control of the hospital she was given the power to confirm their commander and remained the superior of the order and their chaplains. In a striking ceremony, members of the order professed their vows to the Abbess, proclaiming her as "my Prelate and my Lady, Superior, Mother and legitimate administratrix in spiritual and temporary affairs."[171]

Over the centuries, the Abbess accumulated complete ecclesiastical jurisdiction over the territory, villages, and villas subject to Las Huelgas and the Hospital del Rey. An extensive study of the episcopal power exercised by the Abbess appeared in 1944 by none other than Josemaria Escriva de Balaguer, the founder of Opus Dei.[172] In his *La Abadesa de Las Huelgas*, Balaguer details the various powers exercised by the abbesses. In the interests of time, I will merely catalogue the examples of episcopal power documented by Balaguer.

The abbess had complete power over the chaplains assigned to the convent and to the Hospital del Rey attached to the convent. She had exclusive right to assign benefices to the chaplains. She could judge the behavior of the chaplains and remove them and even jail them for improper behavior. Not only could she appoint and discipline the chaplains, however. She also had the power to appoint parish priests for the countryside subject to the convent of Las Huelgas. This involved some sixty-four villages. She could establish new curates and benefices. She could unite benefices or parochial Churches; transfer benefices from closed Churches or reopen closed Churches. She could approve confessors for all her subjects and examine their credentials if necessary. Curates appointed by the abbess could not only hear the confessions of those under her care, but also the confessions of pilgrims and strangers. They could also absolve cases reserved for bishops whenever the abbess authorized them to do so.[173]

Apart from and alongside the power the abbess had over her own clergy, she also had the power to confer licenses to say Mass, or to hear confessions or to preach in those areas subject to her control. She could punish or confront any preacher in her diocese if he was preaching heresy. She had the authority to authorize her subjects to proceed to Holy Orders, to grant letters dimissory,[174] and issue wedding licenses. She could give licenses to officiate at marriages but not officiate herself.

No bishop or delegate from the Holy See could perform a visitation of the churches or altars or curates or clerics or benefices under the care of the abbess. She could recognize and implement any dispensations that came from Rome to her diocese or district. She could commute last wills and testaments when there was just cause. She had the power to visit and examine the adequacy of the apostolic, imperial, or royal notaries, and if she found them delinquent in their duties she could punish them or prohibit them from office. She had the authority to reserve cases regarding her subjects, just like other bishops.

She had the faculty by means of ecclesiastical judges chosen by her to impose censures and prohibitions. She could dispense her nuns from their vows as well as dispense her ecclesial and regular subjects from the Divine Office. She could punish any secular person who broke the law. Finally, the Abbess of Las Huelgas was able to convene a synod in her diocese and to make synodal constitutions and laws for both her religious and lay subjects.

One or all of the extraordinary powers of Las Huelgas was confirmed by Honorius III in 1219, Gregory IX in 1234, and Innocent IV in 1248 and again in 1252.[175] Not that there were not occasional challenges to the power of the abbess. In 1622, for instance, Gregory XV issued the bull Inscrutabili requiring the approval of bishops for confessors and preachers both in parishes and in houses of religious orders, including those ordinarily exempt, in an attempt to implement the decrees of the Council of Trent. Ana of Austria, the Abbess of Las Huelgas, requested that the pope "clarify" his decree in regard to her powers. To quote Elizabeth Connor's astute account of the affair: "[The Pope] assured the Abbess that the Regulations of the decrees of the Council of Trent did not revoke her authority, and he confirmed her privileges of exemption and immunity, and reaffirmed her spiritual and temporal jurisdiction."[176]

Finally, in 1873, after seven hundred years, Pius IX in his decree *Quae diversa*, put an end to the episcopal powers of the Abbesses of Las Huelgas. The Abbess, Dona María del Pilar Ugarte, mounted a spirited legal defense, but to no avail. On February 1, 1874, she wrote to the daughterhouses of Las Huelgas informing them that Las Huelgas was now under the jurisdiction of the Bishop of Burgos.[177]

Was Las Huelgas unique in its exercise of episcopal powers? Again, much more work needs to be done here, but at least for the period before the Fourth Lateran Council in 1215, Las Huelgas does not appear to be an exception. According to Maria Filomena Coelho in her recent study *Expresiones Del Poder Feudal: El Cister Femenino En Leon*, the Cistercian abbesses in Spain installed the chaplains for the churches subject to their monasteries in a ritual in which the chaplains professed their obedience to the abbess for life in front of the entire community.[178] The statutes from 1257 that Coehlo quotes here also indicate that the abbesses professed their own nuns. Unfortunately, she provides no further discussion of the ecclesiastical authority of the abbesses.

Similar powers were exercised by convents in other parts of Europe. To quote Connor, "The Abbess of Las Huelgas was not the only abbess to enjoy jurisdictional powers in the Middle Ages. Several other of the more famous ones were the Abbesses of Jouarre and Fountevraud in France, of Quedlingbourg and Essen in Germany, and of the Cistercian monastery of Conversano in Italy, where the Abbess wore a mitre and members of the clergy prostrated before her."[179]

Was this power "real" episcopal power or, as Balaguer would describe it, quasi-episcopal power? The answer to this question depends on what one considers a "real" bishop to be. There seems little question that the Abbess of Las Huelgas performed most of the administrative roles that a "real" bishop would. One imagines, in fact, that very few bishops were powerful enough to attain an exemption from the implementation of the Council of Trent. The more central question would seem to be what, if any, sacramental functions the Abbess of Las Huelgas or her contemporaries might have performed. As described already, significant evidence exists that abbesses did indeed lead liturgies, hear confessions, and read the Gospel.

In case of Las Huelgas, however, no less an authority than Pope Innocent III recorded instances of liturgical services performed by the Abbess of Las Huelgas. In 1210, he thundered out against these abuses:

> *News of certain things recently have reached our ears, about which we are not a little amazed, that abbesses, namely those constituted in the diocese of Burgos and Palencia, bless their own nuns, and hear the confessions of sins of these same, and reading the Gospel presume to preach publicly. Since then this is equally incongruous and absurd (nor supported by you to any degree), we order through the apostolic writing at your discernment so that, lest this be done by others, you take care by the apostolic authority firmly to prevent [these actions] because even though the most blessed virgin Mary was more worthy and more excellent than all of the apostles, yet not to her, but to them the Lord handed over the keys to the kingdom of heaven.[180]*

There is little doubt that the abbesses mentioned here include the Abbess of Las Huelgas and those of her daughter convents since they were (and are) in Burgos and Palencia. While Innocent wrote as if the actions of the abbesses were unheard of innovations, in fact abbesses had been hearing confessions, reading the Gospel, and preaching for centuries.

During these early centuries, it must be noted, confession and penance had not yet been defined as sacraments, nor were they clearly differentiated from spiritual direction and yet, given this understanding of penance, abbesses heard confessions and gave penance in the same way as priests and bishops of the time.

Not until the end of the twelfth century would ecclesiastical officials begin to insist that only priests could preach; indeed, Hildegard of Bingen went on a famous preaching tour to reform the morals of the clergy.[181] The reading of the Gospel by abbesses, despite Innocent's dire warning, was a regular occurrence in the twelfth century, so much so that a number of twelfth-century theologians and canonists, most notably the infamous Abelard and his learned wife, Heliose, insisted that abbesses were also deaconesses and so authorized to read the Gospel.[182]

Carthusian nuns, in fact, continued to receive a stole as part of their consecration rite until 1975. Abbesses in particular wore the stole for the reading of the Gospel during matins when a priest was not available to do so.[183] This practice would appear to have come from the ordination rites for a deaconess in the tenth through twelfth centuries, where the deaconess also received a stole as a sign of her commission to read the Gospel.[184]

Abbesses, then, performed many of the liturgical functions later reserved for priests and bishops. They were considered by themselves and by their contemporaries to be ordained ministers and, as such, were able to perform sacramental functions. Their sacramental ministry was not the same as that of a priest or a bishop; they did not, for instance, ordain priests. This would make sense, though, since they did profess their own nuns just as a bishop would ordain his own priests.

More could, and should, be said here, especially about the change in the definition of ordination that took place in the eleventh and twelfth centuries, a change that excluded women from many, if not most, liturgical functions.[185] However, the purpose of this presentation was merely to present the case that women played a much more significant role in the liturgical and administrative functions of the Church for the first twelve hundred years of its history. And that raises the important and intriguing question: If they have played such roles in the past, can they not play such roles in the future?

NOTES

140. Kevin Madigan, and Carolyn Osiek, *Ordained Women in the Early Church: A Documentary History* (Baltimore: Johns Hopkins Press, 2005), 195, with English translation.

141. Ibid., 195–96 and Georgio Otranto, *"Note sul sacerdozio femminile nell'antichità in margine a una testimonianza di Gelasio I."* *Vetera Christianorum* 19 (1982): 341–60. English translation in Mary Ann Rossi, "Priesthood, Precedent, and Prejudice: On Recovering the Women Priests of Early Christianity." *Journal of Feminist Studies in Religion* 7 (1991): 73–93. This discussion appears on 88–89, and idem, *"Il sacerdozio della donna nell'Italia meridionel,"* *Italia meridionel e Puglia paleochristiane: Saggi storici. Scavi e ricerche,* 5 (Bari: Edipuglia, 1991), 114–15.

142. Council of Nîmes, c. 2, in Charles Munier, ed., *Concilia Galliae,* Corpus christianorum, series latina, 148. Turnhout: Brepols, 1963, 50.

143. Joseph Ysebaert, "The Deaconesses in the Western Church of Late Antiquity and Their Origin," in G. M. Bartelink, A. Hilhorst and C. H. Kneepkens, eds., *Eulogia: Mélange offerts à Antoon A. R. Bastiaensen à l'occasion des son soixante-cinquième anniversuire,* (Instrumenta patristica, 24. Steenbruge: Abbatia S. Petri, 1991), 428–29; Aimé George Martimort, *Les Diaconesses: Essai historique* (Rome: Edizione Liturgiche, 1982). English translation: *Deaconesses: An Historical Study.* San Francisco: Ignatius Press, 1986), 193–94 and Madigan and Osiek, *Ordained Women,* 184 read this as deaconal rather than presbyteral.

144. *Epistola 14,* in *Epistolae Romanorum pontificum genuinae et quae ad eos scriptate sunt a S. Hilaro usque ad Pelagium II,* ed. Andreas Thiel (1867; reprint New York: Georg Olms Verlag, 1974), 376–77.

145. Otranto, "Priesthood," 83.

146. Letter of Bishops Licinius, Melanius, and Eustochius, in *Les Sources de l'Histoire du Montanisme,* ed. Pierre de Labriolle, Collectanea Friburgensia, n.s., 15 (Fribourg: Librairie de l'Université, 1913). Translation from Madigan and Osiek, *Ordained Women,* 188.

147. Ibid.

148. *Epistola 7, Zachariae Papae Ad Pipinum Majorem Domus, Itemque Ad Episcopos, Abbates, et Proceres Francorum*, Jacques Paul Migne, ed. *Patrologiae cursus completus...Series Latina.* 217 vols. (1844–1865, reproduced Cambridge: Chadwyck-Healey, 1996–2006) 89: 933C. Translation in Ute Eisen, *Women Officeholders in Early Christianity: Epigraphical and Literary Studies* (Collegeville, MN: Liturgical Press, 2000), 133–34.

149. Council of Paris, 829, c. 45, in *Concilia aevi Karolini (742–842)*, ed. Albert Werminghoff, MGH, Concilia 2,1 (Hannover: Hahn, 1907), 639. Translation by Haye van der Meer, *Women Priests in the Catholic Church: A Theological-Historical Investigation*, (Philadelphia: Temple University Press, 1973), 95.

150. Werminghoff, *Concilia aevi Karolini*, 639. Translation by van der Meer, *Women Priests*, 96.

151. The texts are discussed in Jean Leclerq, "Eucharistic Celebrations Without Priests in the Middle Ages," *Worship* 55 (1981):160–65.

152. The text is a copy of a Communion service for men contained in a psaltery copied at Montcassino under Abbot Odesius (1097–1105). The service from Montcassino has been edited by André Wilmart, *"Prières pour la Communion en deux psautiers du Mont-Cassin," Ephemerides liturgicae,* 43 (1929): 320–28.

153. The text has been edited by Jean Leclercq, *"Prières médiévales pour recevoir l'eucharistie pour saluer et pour béner la croix," Ephemerides liturgicae* 79 (1965): 327–40.

154. Leclerq, "Eucharistic Celebrations," 165.

155. Ibid., 165.

156. Ibid., 163.

157. C. 22 of *Vita Odiliae Abbatissae Hohenburgensis*, in Bruno Krusch and Wilhelm Levison, eds., *Passiones vitaeque sanctorum aevi merovingici*, Monumenta Germaniae Historica, Scriptorum rerum Merovingicarum, 6 (Hannover: Hahn, 1913), 50.

158. For a thorough analysis of confession to the abbess or her delegate within the convent, see Gisela Muschiol, *Famila Dei: Zur Liturgie in merowingischen Frauenklöstern, Beiträge zur Geschichte des alten Mönchtums und des Benediktinertum*, 41 (Munster: Aschendorff, 1994), 222–63. For a recent discussion of the practice of penance in the early Middle Ages, see Sarah Hamilton, *The Practice of Penance: 900–1050* (Woodbridge, Suffolk: Boydell Press, 2001). Theologians into the thirteenth century continued to argue that laity, including women, had the power to hear confessions. See Paul Laurain, *De l'intervention des laiques, des diacres et des abbesses dans l'administration de la pénitence* (Paris: Lethielleux, 1897) and Georg Gromer, *Die Laienbeicht im Mittelalter: Ein Beitrag zu ihrer Geschichte, Veröffentlichungen aus dem Kirchenhistorischen Seminar München*, 7 (Munich: Lentnerschen, 1909).

159. See *"De assidue danda confessione,"* and c. 7 *"De non manifestandis sororum confessionibus,"* Waldebert of Luxeuil, *Regula ad virgines*, c. 6, *PL* 88:1059A–1660C and *"Qualiter ad confessionem omnibus diebus ueniant,"* Doñatus of Besançon, *Regula ad virgines*, c. 23 in Adalbert de Vogüé, "La Règle de Doñat pour l'Abbesse Guthstrude," *Benedictina*, 25 (1978), 266. The *Rule* dates from the seventh century; see Muschiol, *Famula Dei*, 10–15.

160. See cc. 18–20, Waldebert, *Regula ad virgines*, *PL* 88: 1067B–1068C, and cc. 69–71, Doñatus, *Regula ad virgines*, de Vogüé, "La Regle," 304–5.

161. C. 6 of *Vita Bertilae Abbatissae Calensis*, in *Passiones vitaeque sanctorum aevi merovingici*, ed. B. Krusch and W. Levison, MGH, *Scriptorum rerum Merovingicarum*, 6 (Hannover: Hahn, 1913), 106.

162. C. 25 of *The Life of St. Ite, Virgin* in *Vitae sanctorum Hiberniae*, ed. Charles Plummer, 2 vols. (Oxford: Clarendon, 1910), 2:125. The second penance occurs in c. 38, ibid., 129.

163. Eisen, *Women Officeholders*, 201–5, has a complete description of the evidence for Theodora as well as an English translation of the inscriptions.

164. Eisen, *Women Officeholders*, 199–200. She also includes an English translation of the inscription.

165. Madigan and Osiek, *Ordained Women*, 193. The inscribed stone now exists in the Basilican Cemetery of St. Paul's in Rome and Madigan and Osiek assume a Roman origin. They do not discuss Eisen's identification of the inscription as Umbrian. They also include an English translation of the inscription.

166. C. 19 in *Bethu Brigte*, ed. Donncha Ò hAodha, (Dublin: Dublin Institute for Advanced Studies, 1978), 6. The translation is that given by Ò hAodha, 24.

167. The tombstone of Mathilda, daughter of Otto I, describes her as *metropolitana* and abbess of Quedlinburg. *Metropolitanus* is commonly used for a bishop and so may indicate that Mathilda played such a role. See Edmund Stengel, "Die Grabschrift der ersten Abtissin von Quedlinbug," *Deutches Archiv für Geschichte des Mittelalters* 3 (1939): 36–70.

168. "*Quando ordinatur abbatissa uestitur a deo uotis in sacrario ueste religionis et inponitur ei in capite mitra religiosa; et precedentes ac subsequentes eam alie deo uote cum cereis, tacentes ueniunt ad corum. Adplicans tamen eam episcopus ad altare, cooperit eam pallio per caput, et dicit super eam hanc orationem:*

Oratio. Omnipotens domine deus aput quem non est discretio sexuum, nec ulla sanctorum disparilitas animarum; qui uiros ad spiritalia certamina corroboras, ut feminas non relinquas: pietatem tuam humili supplicatione deposcimus, ut huic famule tue, quam sacrosancto gregi uirginum nostrarum inpositio[ne] manuum, et hoc uelaminis tegumento (covering; defense) in cenobio (monstery) matrem, fieri preobtamus, clementia tua roboratrix adueniat et adiutrix perpetuo non recedat. [D]a ei domine fortitudinem spiritalia bella gerenda, ut condam debbore bellatrici, procinctum certaminis contra sisare hostilem cuneum tribuisti. Ut sicut ducatu illius sraelitici populi aduersarii preire ita uigilantia huius multitudo daemonum [que] aduersus animas sanctas cotidie dimicatur et militat, uirtute tua penitus disturbetur et pereat. Adsit ei tua dextera consolatrix, que iudit uidue in perniciem non defuit olofornis. Ita domine sermonibus piis et tui adiutorio nominis exterminet usquequaque satan, ut estor humilis infestum tuis plebibus exterminauit aman. Doña ei domine castimoni9 custodiam indefessam, et karitatis sincerissimam dulcedinem gratiosam. Sit sollers in creditarum sibi regimine animarum, et celer in suarum correctione culparum. Ita subditas sibi spiritali zelo coerceat, et materne pietatis affectu refobeat, [ut] nec blanditia dissolute, nec nimia coercione reddantur pusillanimes aut proterue. Da ei christe domine spiritum discretionis ommimodae ut nec onesta dilaceret, nec inonesta delectetur. Atque ita te inluminante sibi creditam multitudinem tuo sancto nomini iugiter admonendo faciat inseruire, ut quum nube fla[m]miuoma mundum ueneris iudicare postrema subditarum profectibus gloriosa, et de nullius perditione confusa, tuae genetricis adiungatur gloriosa cetibus letabunda cum suis omnibus feliciter coronanda. Amen. Te prestante.

Qua explicita osculatur eam episcopus, et tradit ei librum regule et baculum. Ac post salutat oepiscopus et dicit diaconus: Missa acta est." José Janini, ed., *Liber ordinum episcopal [Cod. Silos, Arch. Monástico, 4]*, Studia silensia, 15 (Burgos: Abadia de Silos, 1991), 101–2.

169. "*PALLIUM,...Concil. Tolet. X. can. de viduis : Ut autem nihil devocetur in dubium, Pallio purpuei vel nigri coloris caput contegat ab initio susceptae religionis.*" Charles DuCange, ed., *Glossarum mediae et infirmae latinitatis* (1883–87. Reprint. Graz: Akademische Druck-U. Verlagsanstalt, 1954), 5:34.

170. Janini, *Liber ordinum*, 997–98.

171. For a brief history of Las Huelgas, see Elizabeth Connor, "The Royal Abbey of Las Huelgas and the Jurisdiction of its Abbesses," *Cistercian Studies*, 23 (1988): 128–55. This quote is from p. 144.

172. Josemaria Escriva de Balaguer, *La Abadesa de Las Huelgas: Estudio teologico juridico*, 2nd ed. (Madrid: Ediciones Rialp, 1974). The first edition appeared in 1944, and a third edition appeared in 1988. I have not seen the third edition, but the second varies from the first only in the addition of a second preface.

173. The powers of the abbesses are described and documented by Balaguer in chapter 6 of *La Abadesa*, pp. 135–162.

174. Letters given by a bishop dismissing a person who is moving into another diocese and recommending him for reception there.

175. Connor, "The Royal Abbey," 150.

176. Ibid., 151.

177. Ibid., 152–3.

178. Maria Filomena Coelho, *Expresiones Del Poder Feudal: El Cister Femenino En Leo* (León: Universidad de León, 2006), 154. See also 154, n. 136.

179. Connor, "The Royal Abbey," 146.

180. Book 5, t. 38, c. 10, in Emil Friedberg, ed., *Corpus iuris canonici,* 2 vols. (Graz: Akademische Druck-und-Verlagsanstalt, 1959): 2: 886–87; English translation from Bernard Cooke and Gary Macy, eds., *A History of Women and Ordination,* vol. 2, Ida Raming, The *Priestly Office of Women: God's Gift to a Renewed Church* (New York: Scarecrow Press, 2004), 143n8.

181. See, for instance, F. Doñald Logan, *A History of the Church in the Middle Ages* (London: Routledge, 2002), 177.

182. For a complete discussion of this issue, see Gary Macy, *The Hidden History of the Ordination of Women* (New York: Oxford University Press, 2007), 93–98.

183. "*Actuellement, elles comprennent tout d'abord des rites, au cours de la consécration des vierges accomplie selon le Pontifical romain : l'évêque remet à chaque moniale successivement le manipule, l'étole et une croix en prononçant une formule adaptée après le chant d'une antienne par le choeur. Elles comportent aussi deux privilèges canonico-liturgiques : le droit pour les moniales consacrées de chanter l'épître à la messe conventuelle solennelle, et celui de chanter l'évangile à matines, revêtues de l'étole. en cas d'absence de prêtre, cela jusqu'en 1975. On note que l'étole se porte alors selon mode des prêtres, qui est aussi celui des anciennes diaconesses, et non selon celui diacre.*" Augusin Devaux, *Études et documents pour l'histoire des Chartreux,* Analecta Cartusiana, 208 (Salzburg: Institut für anglistik und amerikanistik Universität Salzburg, 2003), 28.

184. On the ordination of deaconesses, see Macy, *The Hidden History,* 70–73, 131–142.

185. On the important change in the understanding of what constitutes ordination, see Macy, *The Hidden History.*

5. Women of the Catholic Reformation and Early Modern Period

Eileen C. Burke-Sullivan, STD, Assistant Professor of Theology and Director of the Master of Arts in Ministry Program
Creighton University

Others again have propounded reasons why there are more supersti-tious women found than men. And the first is, that they are more credulous; and since the chief aim of the devil is to corrupt faith, therefore he rather attacks them. The second reason is, that women are naturally more impressionable, and more ready to receive the influence of a disembodied spirit.... The third reason is that they have slippery tongues, and are unable to conceal from their fellow-women those things which by evil arts they know; and, since they are weak, they find an easy and secret manner of vindicating themselves by witchcraft. All wickedness is but little to the wickedness of a woman. And to this may be added that, as they are very impressionable, they act accordingly.

There are also others who bring forward yet other reasons... they are feebler both in mind and body, [so] it is not surprising that they should come more under the spell of witchcraft. For as regards intellect, or the understanding of spiritual things, they seem to be of a different nature from men; a fact which is vouched for by the logic of the authorities, backed by various examples from the Scriptures.... Women are intellectually like children.....

But the natural reason is that she is more carnal than a man, as is clear from her many carnal abominations. And it should be noted that there was a defect in the formation of the first woman, since she was formed from a bent rib, that is, a rib of the breast, which is bent as it were in a contrary direction to a man. And since through this defect she is an imperfect animal, she always deceives...And it is clear in the case of the first woman that she had little faith; And all this is indicated by the etymology of the word; for femina comes from fe and minus, since she is ever weaker to hold and preserve the faith. And this as regards faith is of her very nature...a wicked woman is by her nature quicker to waver in her faith, and consequently quicker to abjure the faith, which is the root of witchcraft [186]

In 1486, two Dominican members of the Inquisition of the Catholic Church, under the directive of Pope Innocent VIII, began a tragic period of ecclesial and civil violence that quickly spread beyond the Roman Church to Protestant communities. All across Northern Europe, the British Isles, and the British colonies of North America, a witch-hunt began which largely targeted women. The most vulnerable were women who were poor, had birth defects or skin diseases, who raised gardens of medicinal herbs, or who for various reasons did not marry or were widowed. Over a 150-year period, some 200,000 people had been tortured and burned at the stake for being witches. The majority were women. While the original impetus came from the Church's Inquisition, later the Inquisition leaders tried to put a stop to the madness that was by then driven by local courts and communities, especially in the German states, which had no central courts. For many ordinary women, this irrational explosion of misogyny was the most immediate reality of the period of the Renaissance and Reformation.[187]

Few periods of Western Civilization have been as dynamic or as dangerously violent as the 200-year span from the late fifteenth century until the late seventeenth century. The Dickensian phrase "it was the best of times, it was the worst of times" could as aptly be applied to these years as it was to the period of the French Revolution 100 years later.

Change is the byword of the Renaissance/Reformation and Early Modern periods of Western history. The Copernican discovery of the relationship between the planets, followed by the invention of the telescope, enabled the study of the sun and other stars, the moon, and other celestial bodies. This set off a long period of developing knowledge about the created order that threatened the religious convictions of the time. On the social and political fronts, new kinds of political structures were emerging in Europe, new lands and peoples were discovered and conquered, and new possibilities for wealth and power emerged. The invention of the printing press in the fifteenth century opened education and social advancement to ordinary people, so that the middle class of merchants and craftsmen that developed in the high Middle Ages now expanded and became a striking social force. Painting, art, music, drama, architecture, and entertainment became available to the ordinary public as well as the nobility. The focus of philosophy, arts, and literature turned toward the glory and the beauty of the human person.

New theories of the created order, of the meaning and purpose of human life, of the causes of illness and disease, and of the right relationship with God were raised and discussed in virtually every nation. The absolute authority of the Pope and the Catholic Church were successfully challenged in the Protestant Reformation, and new theological ideas were developed and published at remarkable speed for people who had been used to one new idea in a lifetime, not one every day.

The role of women and their influence on the Catholic Church in this period of dramatic social, political, and religious change could not yet be fully illustrated by the so-called ordinary women. The witch craze in Northern Europe created an environment in which few women wanted to be known or recognized. In most countries, the lot of women in regard to education was only beginning to change. It is generally only from a cadre of extraordinary women about whom we have some firsthand data, that we can recognize some of the contributions of women during these years. In this period, much of the literature about women was written by men with the purpose of generally discounting, diminishing, or undermining women's contributions.

One of the most famous scholars of the period, Desiderius Erasmus, wrote a scathing critique of education for women, aimed perhaps at Margaret Roper, the very well-educated daughter of Thomas More. Erasmus argued against the education of women because, he insisted, women were made for sexual pleasure and were not appealing if they manifested intelligence or learning. Further, he insisted that in the service of love that is marriage, all authority was to be in the hands of the husband. "Nature requires the man to be dominant because the woman is always politically subordinate, and he is her natural superior."[188]

Despite such drivel, there were powerful and effective women, dominant women, women who changed the maps of Europe by their very important political and ecclesial decisions. The most obvious long-term cultural movers and shakers were those of extraordinary personal and political power such as Isabella of Castile, Mary Tudor and Elizabeth I of England, Mary of Scotland, and Catherine de Medici of France. All of them influenced the Church positively and negatively in their own times, and some of their decisions continue to influence it to the present.

From a Catholic Church perspective, another group of remarkably able and influential women were the rule breakers who reformed or founded new religious movements, nearly all of which became established religious communities in time. Of these, there is a remarkable list: Teresa of Avila is perhaps most famous and has remained theologically and spiritually influential in the Church. But women such as Angela Merici, Louise de Merillac, Jane Frances de Chantal, and Mary Ward (to name only a few) had followers in the thousands who, down to the present day, have provided often extraordinary ecclesial ministry with little thanks and frequent difficulties from the hierarchy.

A third group of women who had great influence on the Church of this period were talented and at least partially educated women of personal wealth who supported the work of men in reforming the Church. Representative of this category are Leonor de Osorio de Vega and her daughter, Isabel de Vega de Osorio de Luna. Both were wives, mothers, political players with their powerful husbands, and devout Christian women with a mission to assist the poor while developing their own spiritual lives.

If time or space would permit us to do so, it would be important as well to look to the mission lands colonized in the fifteenth and sixteenth centuries and encounter some of the native women who greatly influenced the Catholic faith by their lives or work. Kateri Tekakwitha,[189] the beatified Lily of the Mohawks in North America, and Sor Juana de la Cruz,[190] half-Spanish, half-native-Peruvian poet and scholar who set Europe abuzz with the extraordinary beauty of her writing, provide exemplary insights into the ways the Church (with its grace and its structural sins) expanded in this extraordinary missionary period. Unfortunately, the limitations of this project will not allow space for that exploration here.

Through lives marked by both astonishing successes and tragic failures in the love and service of humanity, every one of these women defy the stupidity, the crudity, and the violence of *Malleus Malificarum* and the snide defensiveness of Erasmus' assertions. We have not time to discuss them all, but let me give a bit of flesh to at least a representation of them.

Isabella of Castile[191]

In the 225 years from 1475 to 1700, a number of women came to the highest temporal power due to various sets of circumstances. While philosophical arguments raged across the universities of Europe about whether women *could* rule, several very important women did, in fact, rule and rule very effectively, influencing their own regional or national history and the development of the Church and the life of faith as well. The names of Mary Tudor, Elizabeth I, Catherine de Medici of France, the Empress Isabel of Spain, wife of Charles V and regent for her son Philip II until he reached majority, are all familiar to readers of history.

Emblematic of this group and something of a grandmother figure for them figuratively, and in some cases literally, was Isabella of Castile, wife of Ferdinand of Aragon and co-ruler of Spain for eighteen years before her death in 1504. Ferdinand went on to reign in both their names for another twelve years—deeply respectful of Isabella's wishes and expectations as he administered the Provinces of Castile along with his own Province of Aragon.

Isabella has been described as remarkably self-educated, religiously devout, somewhat high-strung, occasionally sentimental, rigid in her personal code of purity, and a woman of stout strength of character and determination. She had three options for marriage immediately upon becoming recognized as the heiress of the throne of Castile by her half brother Henry IV in 1467. Alfonso V of Portugal was older and politically stronger; Charles of Valois, younger son of King Charles VII of France, was engaged in dynastic fights of his own; and Ferdinand of Aragon, a year younger than she and heir to the throne of the eastern quarter of the Iberian Peninsula all vied for her hand and her power. She chose Ferdinand, partly because he was in no position to bargain with her since she had the stronger political clout, and because the union between Aragon and Castile was much desired by Ferdinand's father. She could and did dictate the marriage settlement on her terms, which included ruling in fact and not just in name or appearance.

Over time, however, the couple seemed to fall in love and certainly developed a good working friendship. Ferdinand was considered to be intelligent, handsome, charming, and devout. Although not particularly faithful to his wife in his sexual exploits, he was adept at forwarding her interests along with his own throughout their marriage and at receiving her help and leadership for his people when it was appropriate.

After their marriage, they labored on each other's projects with an instinct for finding ways to meet their subjects' needs while furthering the prestige of the crown. Under their joint authority, they celebrated the culmination of the 800-year effort to rid Spain of Muslim rulers (the *Reconquista*) and united Spain into a single political and economic entity, strongly supporting the Catholic Church.

But it was Isabella alone who made the decision to support a soldier-sailor from Genoa, Italy, named Christopher Columbus with money, ships, and a royal commission to sail west to attempt to reach the Indies, thus opening the door to Spain's hegemony in the discovery and colonizing of the New World for the following century. Along with conquering Granada, the last stronghold of Muslim rule on Spanish soil (and throughout much of Europe) and driving all Muslims who did not convert out of Spain, Isabella, in a less brilliant and darkly backward-thinking move, also disenfranchised the long-established Jewish community of Castile and forced them to convert to Christianity or leave Spain en masse in 1492.

Despite this cruel and oppressive decision in regard to Muslims and Jews, she and Ferdinand were passionately interested in justice for their Christian subjects and developed a revolutionary court system that was organized to support a more just social order. After years of civil war with a noble class who often treated the citizenry with contempt and cruelty, the Catholic monarchs united their people in the common cause of land reform, court establishment, better trade with neighboring countries, and the benefits of years free from local strife and political violence.

Isabella also took her role as a Catholic monarch very seriously and mandated both moral uprightness and better education for the diocesan clergy, better preaching, reform of convents and monasteries, and a universal call to a deepened life of faith among her Christian subjects. Isabella worked closely with the brilliant Cardinal Ximenes de Cisneros to underwrite a polyglot translation of the Bible from original Greek and Hebrew manuscripts and to establish the University of Alcalá specifically for the education of clergy. Before she and Ferdinand had even completed the dynastic struggles early in their reign, they called a council of all the dioceses of Castile and Aragon at Seville and secured the local bishops' support for the royal prerogative of appointing local bishops rather than absentee foreigners who were loyal to the papacy over their people and the crown. This effort was not immediately successful, but by 1486 Innocent VIII (the same one who believed in witches) agreed to the Catholic monarchs' right to appoint bishops for lands of Granada they conquered and subsequently all lands conquered in the name of the Spanish Crown. This was to have a long-term devastating effect on the development of the Church of Latin America. But at the beginning it may have been a good thing, because Isabella was actually more morally ordered than the popes of the time and more attuned to the needs of local dioceses than were the papal legates and the pope. The Spanish monarchs also reduced the absolute wealth of the Church, which in England had proved such a temptation to Henry VIII and induced his rupture with Rome, with its devastating long-term consequences for both ecclesial and civil society in England, Ireland, and Scotland.

The standards of holiness, administrative competence, and theological wisdom in the episcopate rose markedly during the reign of the Catholic monarchs and their initial descendents. The singular efforts of the Catholic monarchs to accomplish a reform of education and morals among the clergy and religious, while not entirely successful, was nonetheless enough to secure the Catholic faith against the inroads of the Protestant Reforms sweeping the rest of Europe by meeting the complaints of the Protestants with a solidly reforming ecclesial community within Spain. Isabella proved to be the opposite of the description of women in the *Malleus Malificarum,* demonstrating that the nature of woman in her intelligence, discipline, and ability to lead is no less than that of any man.

Teresa of Avila[192]

If Isabella was the Catholic monarch who reigned over the dawn of Imperial Spain and inaugurated the reform of Spain's Church, which preceded by a half century the Catholic renewal eventually brought about by the Tridentine reforms, Teresa of Avila is perhaps the emblem of the fullness of that early reform.

Born in Avila in central Spain in 1515, Teresa de Cepeda y Ahumada was the granddaughter of a *Converso*, a Jew who chose to convert to Christianity (or who had already become a Christian) when the Jews were required to become Christian or leave Spain in 1492. Teresa was the third of ten children born to her parents. There were also two older children in the family from Alonso Cepeda y Ahumada's first marriage. Alonso was a wool merchant in the very prosperous trade of Castile. Teresa's mother, Beatriz, a member of one of the older noble families of Avila, had married Alonso when she was only fourteen years old. She died at the age of thirty-three giving birth to her last child. Teresa was just ten at the time of her mother's death and turned to the Blessed Mother for consolation and courage.

Teresa had a reputation for beauty and vivacity. She had many friends, and frequently entertained whole cohorts of cousins and friends with her lively humor. She taught herself to read and write as a small child, and in her teens was sent to a convent finishing school to prepare to be "a perfect wife," according to the description of a Spanish theologian. Illness caused her to be sent home, and as part of her recovery she spent time with a very pious priest uncle who had her read the writings of the Fathers of the Church to him. As she read them, she nearly memorized their content. She made up her mind to enter the Convent of the Incarnation near her home in Avila.

Teresa's story of growing mystical gifts, leadership ability, and determination to reform the Carmelite convents of Spain has been told at length in many places. When one reads her story in the context of her era, however, her accomplishments are simply astonishing. We take for granted today, I believe, that the inner life of each person is valuable and to be nurtured. That was virtually heresy in Teresa's day. We take for granted that God can and does act within the lives of individuals. Again, that would have smacked of heresy in Teresa's day—it sounded too much like what Luther was teaching (it was!) and allowed far too much freedom to ordinary Christians .

The strength of Teresa's personality and her ability to convince friends and enemies alike that God was directing was a *tour de force*. It helped, of course, that King Philip II supported her reform of the Carmelite monasteries and convents and that Teresa was asking for and witnessing to a more demanding life of poverty, discomfort, and enclosure, so that some of the ecclesial leadership likewise supported her. It helped also that Teresa was politically astute and carefully cultivated friends in high places to further the vision of reform she sought to implement.

In all, she established seventeen monastic houses for women and, with John of the Cross, established nearly as many monasteries for men. She was constantly under the shadow of the Inquisition, but despite their harassment completed six major spiritual texts, wrote hundreds of letters that are still extant, and a number of short talks for her sisters on the spiritual life. She was as authentically a friend and spiritual guide for the wealthy and powerful as well as for the women in the scullery. The ecclesial hierarchy more often impeded her work than supported it, and numerous Church leaders would have seconded the words of Filippo Sega, the Papal Nuncio to Spain in 1578, who described her as "an unstable, restless, disobedient and contumacious female who in the name of devotion devised false doctrines, leaving the enclosure against the orders of the Council of Trent and her superiors; and teaching as if she were a master, in spite of St Paul's order that women should not teach."[193]

Sega's words were to become somewhat prophetic in a way that he certainly would never have predicted or been happy about. She died in October 1582. She was canonized with Ignatius Loyola and Francis Xavier in 1622 and declared a doctor of the Church (the first woman to hold such a title) by Pope Paul VI in 1970. Few men or women have had a greater influence on the spiritual life of the Church in the Modern era.

Mary Ward[194]

A considerably less well-known woman founder is an Englishwoman named Mary Ward. The Church owes her a great debt for her ability to translate the seminal spiritual insights of the founder and first general of the Jesuits, Ignatius of Loyola, into a pattern of apostolic, communal life for women that enabled them to serve both the Church and the world outside the cloister. Born of English Catholic nobility in 1585, Mary was raised in an Elizabethan England increasingly inimical to Catholics. Shortly before her birth, acts of Parliament made it treasonous to be a Catholic priest or to hold the Catholic faith. Well-educated in the humanities in a Renaissance home, she was forced to flee to the European continent to follow a vocation in religious vows.

Related by blood or marriage to most of the Catholic aristocracy of England, Mary attracted many of the daughters of these families to join her in the effort to establish a women's community that was like the Jesuits "in all things except those reserved to Holy Orders," according to the formula of the institute that eventually emerged. Consequently, the women of the community she founded were exceedingly well educated in theology, mathematics, language, the arts, rhetoric, and all humane letters. They served by educating girls and women not only to read, write and guide a household, but to run small businesses, nurse the sick, provide spiritual direction, care for the mentally ill, and comfort the brokenhearted. In their native England, the "English Ladies" also disguised themselves as maids, housekeepers, widows, and craftmakers to move through the households of both the wealthy and the poor, to go where priests could not linger, and to draw back into faith many who had fallen away.

Mary's spiritual journey was nurtured and guided by Jesuits as she grew wiser in the skills of discernment and more courageous in following what she discerned. But her life and work were also characterized by official rejection by the Jesuit order she sought to imitate. Worst of all, she suffered frequent, harsh persecutions by members of the Catholic hierarchy—even those who admired her and believed her call to be authentically from God.

It was clear to her that the capacity to serve in every graced aspect of the human enterprise belonged also to women. In one of her frequently quoted talks to novices, she asserted,

> *Therefore I must and ever will stand for this verity[195]: that women may be perfect and the fervor must not necessarily decay because we are women. Women may be perfect as well as men, if they love verity and seek true knowledge....Some, thinking we are women and aiming at greater matters than was ever thought women capable of, they expect perhaps to see us fail, or fall short, in many things....Yet you see many learned men who are not perfect because they practice not what they know, nor perform what they preach. But to attain perfection, knowledge of verity is necessary, to love it and to effect it."[196] By 'verity' Mary means God's truth, belonging neither to men nor to women exclusively, but given to all humans equally by God "to profit yourselves and others.*

Unfortunately, neither the Church nor European temporal society was prepared for women to take on "greater matters" by taking such an active role in the service of faith or development of culture outside the home or cloister. The competence and talent of her community of well-educated women of many nationalities and social strata laboring together outside of the cloister sent a distinct shock through both the Church and the states of early modern Europe. Significant resistance from the political and social cultures across Europe brought great suffering to her throughout the remainder of her life and upon those who were brave enough to cling to her vision and model of community well after her death.

In 1630, Mary's community was officially suppressed by "the harshest [papal] Bull ever to emanate from Rome."[197] Mary was charged with (but never granted a trial or hearing for) heresy, schism, and rebellion, and her enemies in Rome passed the rumor around that she had been, or was about to be, burned at the stake. In fact, she was imprisoned in the sick room of a Poor Clare convent outside of Munich for several months.

Despite being suppressed by the Church, many of Mary's community found a way to remain together as laywomen and then to be recognized as a religious order some years later. The community continues to thrive on five continents under the title of the Institute of the Blessed Virgin Mary but is generally known as the English Ladies. In 2004, the Roman branch was able to finally claim the name Mary Ward had insisted was God's will for her institute: the Congregation of Jesus. The educational and spiritual work of this congregation throughout the world continues as they prepare to celebrate their four hundredth anniversary in 2009.

Mary's collection of writings is relatively small, but it demonstrates her command of language, history, theology, and spirituality. Her journals, retreat notes, letters, and instructions to her sisters, along with the formula for her institute, have been gathered, collected, translated, and commented upon in several languages. They offer a voice interpreting Ignatian spirituality of and for women from the early days of the Society's history.

Leonor de Osorio de Vega[198]

Finally, attention should be turned to laywomen who offered great service to the Church through their own personal commitment to service of the Church, religious reform, and care for the poor as well as their ability to influence the male leaders of the Church and civil structures. These women are actually many in number. Their stories are teased out of letters to the bishops, popes, ecclesial leaders, artists, and civil authorities they partnered or married or worked with, fought with, or financed; from the brief historical reports of projects; from tombstones, cemetery, or parish records; and occasionally from written family histories or the occasional oblique reference in praise or condemnation from speeches, prayer journals, or sermons by famous relatives, protégés, enemies, or friends. Their stories are seldom told in full, and the extent of their influence and the often great work they accomplished is little known or appreciated.

Two such women were remarkably powerful in both the ecclesial and civil worlds of the late-sixteenth century. Mother and daughter, both married women and wives of wealthy and powerful men, they were also friends and supporters of Ignatius Loyola and the early fathers of the Society of Jesus, that dynamic group of clerics who eschewed women members for various cultural reasons but never eschewed the financial and personal support of women.

In his biography of Charles V, the German historian Karl Brandi spoke at length of the role of Juan de Vega in developing and implementing Charles' imperial policy toward the papacy. In the context of his discussion about this critical political relationship, Brandi mentions that Vega's wife Leonor, an Osorio, "was among the first devoted admirers of Ignatius of Loyola."[199] According to Hugo Rahner, among all of the extant letters to and from Jesuit founder Ignatius of Loyola, the most numerous letters involving a single source are to and from the family of this same Juan de Vega, imperial ambassador to the Vatican for four years, and later vice regent of the kingdom of Sicily for Charles V. A substantial portion of those letters were written to Leonor and the Vegas's daughter and youngest child, Isabel de Vega y de Luña.

Shortly after de Vega's family moved to the palatial ambassador's residence in 1543, he and his family established what was to be a lifelong friendship with Ignatius and the whole Society of Jesus. Both husband and wife were from Spanish noble families, he related through his mother to Ferdinand of Aragon and she through her mother to Isabella of Castile. With other Spanish nobility, they had thrown their full support behind the Hapsburg Charles V, grandson of the Catholic monarchs. The couple lost no time in asking Ignatius to become their confessor and spiritual guide. He, in turn, interested Leonor in his project of rescuing prostitutes from the streets of Rome. She financed Martha House, a living situation for street women and their small children, which provided them with the opportunity to learn some crafts or other skills, get basic medical care and find a decent job, usually as servants, or establish a respectable marriage.

Doña Leonor also provided significant material support to Ignatius and the Jesuits at the Roman College, sending candles during Holy Week and food when the larder was running empty and funding scholarships for poor men who entered the order without family support. In other ways, Doña Leonor assisted Ignatius in quelling anti-Jesuit rumors, intervening in conflicts that would have undermined the Jesuit works in Rome—especially Martha's House—and speaking on behalf of Ignatius's position that no Jesuit should be made a bishop when Pope Paul III wanted to appoint them. On a larger stage, Leonor was able to serve as intermediary and model in a marital conflict between the emperor's daughter, Margaret of Austria and the pope's grandson, Otto Farnese.[200]

After the couple moved to Sicily to become viceroy and vicereine in 1547, Leonor continued to assist the work of the Jesuits by building Martha Houses in Messina and Trapani. She facilitated the reform of the Cistercian women's monastery in Messina and supported all the ministries that the Jesuits were undertaking in Sicily. She financially assisted in the founding of the first Jesuit college in Europe in Messina and established no fewer than four orphanages in the urban areas of Sicily. She received permission from the pope to spend up to five days a month in various convents, both for her own spiritual growth and to assist in the ongoing reform of various religious houses.

Doña Leonor's letters to Ignatius give us a picture of a woman busy about the many charitable works she organized and supported. They also indicate the work of parenting and educating her five children, especially her daughter, often in the long absences of her husband who had to travel on the Emperor's business. We discover she is a woman of her own time and culture, but a woman of intelligence, education, political acumen, managerial skills, prayerful piety, concern for the poorest and most vulnerable, and loyal to family, Church, and friends. Late in 1549, she and her husband were negotiating a marriage of state with a most desirable Spanish suitor for their daughter, but that union fell through. In March 1550, Doña Leonor died at the age of forty.

Isabel de Vega y de Luna

Her daughter, Isabel, in her midteens and being sought as a consort by a number of eligible men, was disconsolate at her mother's death. From her childhood Isabel had worked with her mother in her charitable and reform projects, and like her mother sought spiritual guidance from Ignatius. It was to him she turned for consolation after her mother's death. She continued her mother's work of emotional and material support for the various ministries of the society, especially the college in Messina, and the Martha Houses. Isabel's earliest letters after her mother's death are deeply concerned about a young woman she and her mother had been helping. She wants Ignatius to help the girl find work or a suitable marriage in Rome where her past would not be known.

From the correspondence, one can also see the degree of material support she provided for the Jesuit novitiate and college in Messina. This is going forward at the same time she is struggling to make up her mind about a particularly strong Sicilian suitor, Pedro de Luna, whom her father wants her to marry. She was also deeply imbued with a desire to serve God and wondered if she had a vocation to cloistered religious life. After helping her discern that the latter was not her calling, Ignatius encouraged her to embrace the marriage so eagerly desired by her father the viceroy, which she eventually did, apparently to her own happiness and satisfaction as well as the delight of the poor of Sicily, who were fed on the streets for two weeks before and after the nuptial celebrations from the de Vega and de Luña wealth.

The correspondence continues with the good news of children born and important good works going forward, including intervention with the authorities for the feeding and well-being of prisoners in the city prisons, better services at the hospital for the poor, a school for the children of servants on the estates she and her husband owned, and eventually a second college, this time at Bivona, Sicily, to be run by the Jesuits, which she entirely paid for out of her personal monies. Later it is noted by leaders of the Jesuits that even though Emperor Charles V did not take special notice or offer support for the Jesuits in general, he did provide special support for their colleges and ministries in Sicily at the request of Juan de Vega and his daughter Isabel.[201]

At the death of Ignatius in July 1556, Isabel and the whole de Vega family were devastated. Isabel offered the leaders of the Society of Jesus the use of her own estate home in Bivona for the general congregation to elect a successor (the offer was turned down) and continued her generous good works among the poor until her own untimely death in childbirth with her fourth child in January 1558. Isabel was only 25 years old.

Diego Laínez, the second general of the Jesuits, in recognition of her extraordinary contributions to the work of Ignatius and the Society, had written to Isabel after Ignatius' death, "The whole Society of Jesus will always regard you as its mistress in the Lord, and every General in future will always imitate that readiness to serve the Lord Duke and your Excellency which was shown by our blessed Father Ignatius."[202] At the time of Isabel's death, Pedro de Ribadeniera, one of Ignatius' first companions, wrote to Isabel's father, "Our hearts sincerely sympathize with you in your sorrow, for we too have lost in the Duchess a peerless lady and patroness of the whole Society of Jesus."[203] Not only the Society of Jesus, but the poor of Sicily and Rome lost a true friend and champion.

Conclusion

Many of the women of the Early Modern period, which was marked by the brilliance of the Renaissance, the religious transformations of the Reformation, the astounding economic and political changes of the era of discovery, and the violence of the witch-hunting craze were women of strength, courage, devotion, determination, and intelligence. Perhaps three contributions of women of that period of history significant for women in today's Church are 1) their recognition of the call to personal holiness for every person in relationship with God, 2) their competent use of political acumen, and 3) their determination to open the doors of formal education, first to other women of their social standing and then to the men and women of the poorer social strata. Early modern women experienced the power of God's Spirit directing them personally within their own gendered experience and found ways to describe it for others. Many of these women learned to wield real political power in both the Church and in civil structures, and were often willing to use that power to cooperate with others in enhancing the human condition while bringing about essential moral reform. Wherever women fought for education or labored to educate themselves, they made remarkable contributions to culture, to the Christian faith, to societal development, and the whole of the human body, not just the wealthy and powerful. If they address any message to our own times, it is perhaps their commitment to personal holiness with a concomitant right use of political power for the sake of the common good, and the necessity for education of all persons without gender or racial discrimination.

NOTES

186. *Malleus Maleficarum* (1486) translated by Montague Summers [1928] 1.6. www.sacred-texts.com/pag/mm/ accessed May 2, 2008.

187. Information on this period is available from many recent sources. For a good summary of the witch craze, see Mary T. Malone. *Women and Christianity*, Volume III: *From the Reformation to the Twenty-first century*. Maryknoll, NY. Orbis Books 2003, Malone also lists a number of other sources of information on this and other topics concerning women of this period, subsequently cited as Malone III. An excellent resource for the period is John Merriman, *A History of Modern Europe from the Renaissance to the Present*, 2nd Ed. New York & London: Norton & Co, 2004. 46—220.

188. Malone III, 27–28.

189. There are few good resources on Kateri Tekakwitha. A biography that places her in the context of First Nation Native American culture and customs is by Margaret R. Bunson, *Kateri Tekakwitha: Mystic of the Wilderness*, Huntington, IN: Our Sunday Visitor, 1992. Malone III has a brief summary of her life and relationship to the Ursuline Missionary Marie of the Incarnation, pp 141–143.

190. Two resources for excellent information on Sor Juana's contributions are *Sor Juana Inez de*

la Cruz: Selected Writings, translated and edited by Pamela Kirk Rappaport, Mahwah, NJ: Paulist Press, (Classics of Western Spirituality Series) 2005, and *Octavio Paz* (*Sor Juana: Or, the Traps of Faith*, translated *Margaret Sayers Peden*, New York: Belknap. 1990.

191. Much of the background on Isabella given here is drawn from *J.H. Elliott, Imperial Spain 1469-1716*, London: Penguin, 1963, 1970 and 1990, 15–45.

192. Information on Teresa's life and work is largely drawn from Cathleen Medwick, *Teresa of Avila: The Progress of a Soul*, New York etc: Doubleday, 1999; Malone III 63–84, and *Teresa of Avila, The Interior Castle*, translated by Kieran Kavanaugh, OCD, and Otilio Rodriquez, OCD, with introduction by Kieran Kavanaugh, OCD, 1–29.

193. Medwick, 224.

194. Information on Mary Ward is drawn from *Till God Will: Mary Ward Through Her Writings*, edit. By S. M. Emmanuel Orchard, I.B.V.M., London: Darton, Longman and Todd, 1985. This collection includes such autobiographical writing as journals, meditations for her sisters, instructions for novices and letters from throughout Mary's life. The collection also includes some information from the sisters closest to Mary in her work and life (hereafter referred to as *Till God Will*). Margaret Mary Littlehales, I.B.V.M., *Mary Ward: Pilgrim and Mystic*, Turnbridge Wells, Kent England: Burns and Oates, 1998. Phyllis Zagano, *Woman to Woman: An Anthology of Women's Spiritualities*, Collegeville, MN: Liturgical Press. 1993, 54–62 and Malone III 103–112.

195. Truth, which she later identifies as God.

196. *Till God Will*, 58–59.

197. Little Hales, 213.

198. The primary information on Leonor and her daughter Isabel is drawn from Hugo Rahner, S.J., *St. Ignatius Loyola: Letters to Women*, translated by Kathleen Pond and SAH Weetman, New York, Herder, 1960, new ed New York; Crossroad, 2007, 434. Hereafter identified by *Letters to Women*.

199. Karl Brandi, *Emperor Charles V*. Translated by C. V. Wedgwood, New York, NY: Knopf, 1939, 460. Also quoted and cited in *Letters to Women*, 434.

200. *Letters to Women*, 435–438.

201. Rahner cites a report from Polanco, Ignatius's secretary, to the whole society at the beginning of 1555. *Letters to Women*, 474.

202. From a letter from Diego Lainez to Duchess Isabel de Luna on August 7, 1556 as quoted by *Letters to Women*, 478.

203. From a letter from Pedro de Ribadeniera to Viceroy Juan de Vega in January, 1558 as quoted in *Letters to Women*, 478.

6. Catholic Women in the Nineteenth and Twentieth Centuries

Robert Ellsberg, Editor in Chief, Orbis Books

The distinguished speakers who have preceded me make me wonder about my qualifications for being here. I am not a scholar—neither a historian nor a theologian. I am not equipped to address such topics as the evolution of religious life or the sociology of the family. I can only presume that the plausibility of my inclusion comes from my having written a book about women saints, so that perspective will determine my reflections.

My book, *Blessed Among All Women*, offers reflections on women "saints, prophets, and witnesses" from throughout the Christian era.[204] I was inspired to write it by a serious criticism lodged against my previous book, *All Saints*.[205] A number of women pointed out that, while my list of "saints" was unconventional in drawing on figures far outside the official canon, in at least one respect it was quite traditional. That was in the lopsided ratio of men to women—like the official canon itself, approximately three to one.

With some embarrassment, I recognized the justice of this complaint. The list of saints has of course included many famous women—including Mary Magdalene, Monica, Clare of Assisi, Joan of Arc, and Teresa of Avila. Prominent saints of the nineteenth and twentieth centuries include such figures as Bernadette Soubirous, Maria Goretti, Edith Stein, and Mother Teresa of Calcutta. And yet it is an unavoidable fact that among the wide company of official saints, women are vastly underrepresented.

One could speculate about the reasons for this. Many holy women in history tended to spend their lives in the relative seclusion of the cloister. Perhaps they did not leave writings or generate biographies that extended their reputation to a wider circle. Other reasons might be cited as well. But lurking behind them all lies a deeper fact: The process of canonization, like the general exercise of authority in the Church, has been entirely controlled by men. This has affected not only the selection of saints for canonization, but the interpretation of their lives.

Traditional accounts of women saints—almost always written by men—have tended to emphasize "feminine virtues" of purity, humble service, obedience, or patient endurance. Seldom have women been recognized for questioning authority, for defying restrictive codes and modes of behavior, or for audacity and wit in surmounting obstacles placed in their paths.

Even the labels attached to women saints have reflected a narrow range of categories. Apart from the martyrs, women are generally remembered as "foundresses" of religious orders or as virgins, widows, or occasionally matrons—all terms that derive from their marital status. Such labels elide the range of roles women may have performed, whether as theologians, prophets, healers, visionaries, or trailblazers in the spiritual life.

The lives of saints—whether men or women—are generally marked by their creative response, in faith, to the challenges posed by their particular moment in history. Each saint invented a style of discipleship appropriate to the needs of his or her time. This invention and creativity is a particular motif in the history of women saints, who generally struggled hard to assert their full humanity and to follow where God was calling them even when to do so challenged the prevailing options of the time.

For some, this meant claiming the freedom to remain unmarried; for others, it meant to escape the restrictive enclosure of a convent, to engage in active apostolic work among the poor, or to travel across the world to proclaim the Gospel. Some claimed the authority to write their own community rules, to interpret Scripture in new ways, or simply to describe their own experience of God. Others found in Christ a mandate to oppose slavery, war, and social injustice. Later, in light of their achievements and the space they created for new models of discipleship, such women might be honored as "faithful daughters of the Church." But while they lived, they often endured extraordinary opposition or even persecution. Indeed, in the struggle to follow their vocations—especially if this involved any form of innovation—holy women have typically contended with male authorities who were only too eager to inform them that their visions or desires contradicted the will of God.

The last two centuries have been marked by dramatic and accelerating changes in the role and status of women in the Church and society. The struggle by women to assert their full equality and to challenge patriarchal structures and values has been one of the true signs of the times. In this struggle, it is probably safe to say that more dramatic changes in consciousness and social custom have occurred in the past fifty years than in many preceding centuries.

Catholic women have not always served in the forefront of these movements, but they were not unaffected. The history of female holiness, from the anonymous disciples of the New Testament up to the present, could be told as a story of women who discovered through their relationship with Christ the power to name themselves, to express their identity, and to value their own experience in ways that often set them apart from the roles defined by the Church or the wider culture of their time.

In researching the lives of women saints in the nineteenth century, I was struck by the number who were actually excommunicated in the course of their careers. This is seldom mentioned in their official vitae, which again tend to emphasize traditional values of piety, submission, and obedience. I will mention only two examples.

Blessed Anne-Marie Javouhey

Mother Javouhey (1779–1851) founded the Sisters of St. Joseph of Cluny, an order that undertook mission work in such desperate backwaters of the French Empire as Guadeloupe, Senegal, and Martinique. Her work with emancipated slaves in French Guiana provoked the bitter resentment of white farmers. They found a willing ally in their local bishop, who apparently resented Mother Javouhey's independence and seemed exceptionally eager to believe the worst of her. He sent slanderous reports back to France and eventually excommunicated her. Her sisters learned of this only when the priest at Mass passed over their mother superior's open mouth, refusing to give her Communion. In this fashion, she was deprived of the sacraments for two years.

But it was not her only ordeal at the hands of petty hierarchs. Back in France, her local bishop waged a systematic campaign to wrest control of her congregation. He believed that he, by rights, should be the congregation's superior general. Thus, he claimed the power to rewrite the sisters' constitution, putting himself in control of their finances, making all decisions about their mission work, and even forbidding Mother Javouhey to leave the diocese without his permission. When she resisted these prohibitions, which had no legal basis, he threatened to dissolve her congregation.

By the end of her life, Mother Javouhey had overcome these obstacles; she was regarded not only as a holy servant of God, but as a national hero. As she lay close to death, she heard that her old nemesis, the bishop, had died. "So he's gone in ahead of me, that good bishop," she reflected. "Well, that is correct, that is how it should be. A bishop should always enter first." She urged her sisters to pray for his soul. "We ought to think of His Lordship as one of our benefactors," she said. "God made use of him to try us when as a rule we were hearing around us nothing but praise. That was necessary, for since our congregation was succeeding so well we might have thought we were something if we hadn't had these pains and contradictions."[206]

Mother Javouhey died in 1851. She was beatified nearly a century later, in 1950.

Saint Theodora

Among the recently canonized saints of the Americas is Mother Theodore Guerin (1798–1856), founder of the Sisters of Providence of St. Mary of the Woods. She was remembered for her work in bringing a community of sisters from France to a new mission in the frontier territory of Indiana. Beginning with their foundation in a log cabin in the middle of the forest, the sisters contended with fire, locusts, droughts, and floods as they steadily developed their ministry among the pioneer settlers of the region. And, yet again, the most difficult ordeal of their early years involved relations with their local bishop. Mother Theodore initially described him as "an excellent father." Never, she said, had she found "a heart more compassionate under an exterior so cold."[207] But before long she was describing his temperament as "one of those which makes martyrs of their possessors and still more of those who must put up with them."[208]

The problem, it seems, was that the bishop regarded the community as his personal possession, and he sought to control and mange its affairs in every detail. "I have the greatest aversion to this kind of administration," Mother Theodore wrote. "It seems to me it would keep the sisters in a species of slavery."[209]

The bishop tried to revise the sisters' rule. He tried to force the community to depose Mother Theodore as their superior. He insisted that neither she nor any other sister leave the diocese without his written permission. Claiming the land under their home was his, he announced, "I am the proprietor, spiritual and temporal, of that house."[210] When Mother Theodore resisted his interference, he announced she was no longer a Sister of Providence—he had released her from her vows. He ordered her to leave the diocese and "go elsewhere to hide her disgrace."[211] When her sisters vowed to follow her, he threatened to have them all excommunicated and even to have them pursued by the law.

Fortunately, the story had a happy ending. Just as things were reaching a crisis point, word came that the Vatican had accepted the retirement of the bishop in question and that his replacement was on his way. Under the new bishop's benevolent protection the congregation flourished, and 150 years later Mother Theodore was recognized as a saint.

Time does not permit an adequate review of the experience and emerging roles of Catholic women in the nineteenth and twentieth centuries, nor am I competent to offer such a review. Instead, I would like to reflect on several women of these centuries who particularly interest me, models of spirituality or religious life who seem to draw in distinctive ways on their experience as women.

Cornelia Connelly

Cornelia Connelly (1809–1879), Founder of the Society of the Holy Child Jesus, was born to a wealthy Philadelphia family in 1809. In 1831 she married an Episcopal priest named Pierce Connelly. When his studies convinced him that Catholicism was the true religion, he renounced his Anglican orders and entered the Catholic Church. Cornelia joined him. Although in her conversion, as in many subsequent decisions, Cornelia was to some extent carried along by the tide of her husband's strong will, she too felt a call to holiness. She hoped to discover this in the setting of family life; circumstances dictated that it should come instead through suffering and sacrifice.

In 1839 Cornelia and Pierce, with their three children, were living in rural Louisiana, where they both taught in Catholic schools. A fourth child, Mary Magdalene, died after only seven weeks. Five months later, while this wound was still fresh, their two-year-old son fell into a vat of boiling sugar cane juice and died forty-three hours later. During that time, as all the while she held his scalded body, Cornelia experienced a deep identification with the sorrows of Mary. When the child died on February 2, the feast of the Presentation, Cornelia wrote in her diary, "He was taken into the Temple of the Lord."[212]

Later that year, Pierce confided that he wished to seek ordination as a Catholic priest. Cornelia was stricken. It would mean the break-up of the family and, for her, a lifelong commitment to celibacy. Still the dutiful wife, she tried to believe in the coincidence between her husband's wishes and the will of God. So she agreed to cooperate with her husband's plan. She accepted the trial of the celibate life and remained behind, pregnant with her fifth child, while Pierce went off to Rome to explore the possibilities for his vocation.

Eventually Pierce summoned the family to join him. He had secured an audience with Pope Gregory XVI, who accepted his vocation and cleared the way to his ordination, provided that Cornelia would make a vow of chastity. While Pierce pursued his studies, Cornelia lived with her children in a Sacred Heart convent. Though Pierce visited once a week she was, for all practical purposes, quite alone. Prayer offered little consolation. She wrote, "Incapable of listening or understanding or thinking….I forced my will to rejoice in the greatness of God."[213]

In 1845, Cornelia made the requisite vow and Pierce was ordained. It was not clear what she was now supposed to do. She responded to the invitation of several bishops that she establish a religious congregation in England for the education of girls. Cornelia accepted the challenge, provided she could keep her children with her. And so in 1846 she arrived in England to take over a newly built convent school in Derby.

There were numerous twists and turns in the foundation of this school and the community that attended it, but within a few years Cornelia had achieved some eminence within the English Catholic Church. In 1847 she took religious vows and was formally installed as superior of her congregation, the Society of the Holy Child Jesus. The name reflected her profound devotion to the Incarnation, specifically to the "humbled God" who had revealed himself in the form of a helpless infant. In this spirit she instructed her sisters, "As you step through the muddy streets, love God with your feet; and when your hands toil, love Him with your hands; and when you teach the little children, love Him in His little ones."[214]

Her toil at this point was only beginning. After only three years of this life, a new round of trials began. Pierce had grown restless and dissatisfied with the Catholic priesthood. At first he tried to interfere with and take over Cornelia's congregation. After she asked him please to stay away from her convent, he announced that he was leaving the priesthood and wished her to resume her marital duties. Once again, Cornelia was appalled. Though her husband's will had led her to the religious habit, now that she wore it, it was her own, and she would no longer accept Pierce's word as the Word of God.

When she refused his demand, he brought a suit against her in a high ecclesiastical (Anglican) court. Now a professional anti-Catholic, Pierce painted a lurid picture of his wife being held captive by agents of Rome. Nevertheless, the court decided in Cornelia's favor. Enraged, Pierce retaliated by kidnapping her children and taking them out of the country. She was never to see them again.

Cornelia remained the superior of her congregation for over thirty years. Through her schools in several countries, she did much to advance the education of young women, especially the poor. Nevertheless, Mother Cornelia always bore the weight of her many sorrows. Toward the end of her life she suffered from an excruciating case of eczema that gave her the appearance of a leper—as though, it was said, "she had been scalded from head to foot."[215] It seemed she was revisiting in her illness the experience of her greatest sorrow as well as her deepest identification with the Holy Child. Now it was she who was to be offered in the Temple. On the day before she died, on April 18, 1879, she turned to the nursing sister and exclaimed, "In this flesh I shall see my God."[216]

Through much of life, Cornelia Connelly struggled hard to discern her vocation and her duty as a wife and mother amid the claims and demands others made on her. But when she was certain she had heard God's voice, she stood firm despite the terrible sacrifices this entailed.

Thérèse of Lisieux

One of the most popular and influential saints of modern times was the Carmelite nun Thérèse of Lisieux. Pope John Paul II named her a Doctor of the Church—a remarkable fact, given that her reputation rests almost entirely on a slim memoir, *The Story of a Soul,* published after her death in 1897. The wide influence she enjoyed after death was an ironic contrast with the obscurity in which she passed her short life.

The daughter of a pious watchmaker and his wife, Thérèse was fifteen when she entered the Carmelite convent at Lisieux, where two of her sisters had preceded her. She died of tuberculosis nine years later at the age of twenty-four. It might be supposed that the memory of such a short and uneventful life would remain within the walls of her convent. Instead, her name quickly circled the globe. In response to popular acclamation, her canonization was processed with remarkable speed. She was declared a saint in 1925, just twenty-eight years after her death.

What lay behind this development was the success of her autobiography, in which she described her experience and her distinctive insights into the spiritual life. It is a book that might well have been subtitled "The Making of a Saint," for essentially it is about the path to holiness in everyday life.

Despite the sentimental style of her provincial piety, Thérèse presented herself as a woman possessed of a will of steel. As child, she had set her sights on the goal of sanctity, and she went on to pursue this objective with courageous tenacity. She called her method of spirituality the "Little Way." Simply put, it involved performing her everyday actions and suffering each petty insult or injury in the presence and love of God.

As a teenager, Thérèse had stormed heaven to win acceptance into the Carmelite convent. Once inside, she was not content merely to fulfill the letter of her religious rule. Seemingly driven by an inner sense that little time was available, she tried to accelerate the process of sanctification. Devoting herself body and soul to Christ, she offered her life as a victim of love for the salvation of souls. So acute was her belief in the mystical Body of Christ that she believed each act of devotion, each moment of suffering patiently endured, might be credited to other souls in greater need. By this way, she believed it was possible to transform any situation into a profound arena for holiness and that one might thus, through the effect of subtle ripples, make a significant contribution to transforming the world.

Although outwardly she appeared to be a traditional contemplative nun, the saint she identified with most closely was Joan of Arc, the young maid of Orléans who, in obedience to her private voices, transgressed all conventional models of female sanctity. Thérèse writes of her feeling that she was called to all vocations. She felt a powerful vocation to be a priest—but also a warrior, an apostle, a doctor of the Church, and a martyr. "I would like to perform the most heroic deeds," she wrote. "I feel I have the courage of a Crusader. I should like to die on the battlefield in defense of the Church. If only I were a priest!"[217]

The passage of time has not dulled the challenge of this poignant confession. But ultimately, Thérèse came to realize that her vocation was nothing less than charity itself, a virtue embracing every other vocation. "My vocation is love!...In the heart of the Church, who is my Mother, *I will be love*. So I shall be everything and so my dreams will be fulfilled!"[218] At another point, she described her mission as simply "to make Love loved."

Thérèse woke on the morning of Good Friday 1894 to find her mouth filled with blood—the beginning of a protracted period of agonizing suffering. She wrote her autobiography in the months before her death. During this time, her physical torment was often aggravated by periods of intense spiritual suffering that brought her close, at times, to despair. By continuing to pray and to hold fast to the image of Christ, she eventually passed through this dark night and died at peace.

Though Thérèse's emphasis on "littleness" and meekness could be seen as justifying traditional feminine roles, in fact she demonstrated the potential power that resides in the margins. She showed that everyday life—the chores and encounters that make up most lives, could be an arena for the exercise of heroism and that even a life of obscurity could hold open a path toward spiritual greatness.

Madeleine Delbrêl

Thérèse of Lisieux's spirituality, though expressed in the context of a Carmelite convent, points to a model of religious devotion lived out in the exercise of ordinary life in the world. Among holy women in the twentieth century, an increasing number rejected a conventional religious vocation, choosing instead to find and serve God in the realm of work, family, community, and the ordinary business of life.

One of these was Madeleine Delbrêl, a French lay missionary and activist, the daughter of a railway worker, who was born in 1904. Although she spent her youth as a confirmed atheist, at age twenty-four she became convinced of God's existence and saw no alternative but to dedicate her life to his service. Her conversion was an overwhelming, "bedazzling" experience that marked her forever.

Delbrêl briefly considered becoming a nun, but she ultimately discerned that her vocation was in the world. God might call some people to stand apart, she decided, but "there are those he leaves among the crowds.... These are the people who have an ordinary job, an ordinary household, or an ordinary celibacy. People with ordinary sicknesses, and ordinary times of grieving.... These are the people of ordinary life, the people we might meet on any street."[219] Casting her lot with this anonymous crowd, she declared, "We, the ordinary people of the streets, believe with all our might that this street, this world, where God has placed us, is our place of holiness."[220]

With several friends she conceived the idea of a small lay community dedicated to leading a contemplative Christian life in the midst of the world. For the sake of this vocation she prepared herself for three years with ardent discipline, quietly praying, studying Scripture, and taking courses in social work. In 1933, with the blessing of her spiritual director, she and her companions set forth for Ivry, a working-class city near Paris and a stronghold of the French Communist Party.

From the start, the local pastor had trouble comprehending what these women were up to. Having expected that they would occupy themselves with parish duties, he was perplexed when they seemed more interested in spending time with their Communist neighbors. Delbrêl and her companions were themselves struggling to find their way. In their engagement with the workers, who had been long estranged from the Church, they felt they were undertaking a new kind of missionary work. They called themselves "missionaries without a boat"—not traveling overseas, but crossing the borders of faith to bear witness to the Gospel in friendship and solidarity.

Over time, they won their neighbors' trust. With the outbreak of World War II, the city government even asked Delbrêl to oversee services for refugees flooding the town. She organized soup kitchens, clothing drives, and emergency shelters. In recognition of this service, the Communist government wanted to give her a medal after the war, but she declined the honor.

Delbrêl remained as committed as ever to her essential missionary project, building a bridge between the Church and the secular world. Apart from any other accomplishment, such contact with unbelievers strengthened her own faith, forcing her, as she said, to be more authentic, to think critically, to avoid pious clichés. When asked how she prayed, she described her Prayer of the Agenda. It was simply a heightened awareness of the presence of God in all the ordinary activities of life—whether meeting people, answering the phone, or running errands. In these ordinary circumstances, she insisted, a person could experience the deepest spiritual dimensions of life.

At last, with the arrival of Pope John XXIII ("a tiny miracle of God," as she called him) she lived to see the beginnings of a new season in the Church. In many ways, Delbrêl's spirit was embraced by the Second Vatican Council, especially in its affirmation of the special vocation of the laity. As Delbrêl put it, "We are called to be the visible body of Christ in the midst of the human body of society."[221] In turn, she certainly would have embraced the opening words of Pastoral Constitution on the Church in the Modern World (*Gaudium et Spes*), the final document of the Council, which she did not live to see.

But Delbrêl did not place her hopes in grand and historic events. The most significant events in the universe, she believed, were often small and seemingly *ordinary*:

Each tiny act is an extraordinary event, in which heaven is given to us, in which we are able to give heaven to others. It makes no difference what we do, whether we take in hand a broom or a pen. Whether we speak or keep silent. Whether we are sewing or holding a meeting, caring for a sick person or tapping away at the typewriter. Whatever it is, it's just the outer shell of an amazing inner reality: the soul's encounter, renewed at each moment in which the soul grows in grace and becomes ever more beautiful for her God. Is the doorbell ringing? Quick, open the door! It's God coming to love us. Is someone asking us to do something? Here you are! It's God coming to love us. Is it time to sit down for lunch? Let's go—it's God coming to love us. Let's let him.[222]

Delbrêl died in 1964, two weeks shy of her sixtieth birthday.

Dorothy Day

The spirit of Saint Thérèse was also at work in the final figure I would like to consider: Dorothy Day, founder of the Catholic Worker Movement, who died in 1980 at the age of 83. At the time of her death, it was observed that she was "the most influential, interesting, and significant figure"[223] in the history of American Catholicism. This was an extraordinary statement on behalf of someone who occupied no official position in the Church—indeed, someone whose ideas were almost universally rejected throughout most of her life. The Catholic Worker, a lay movement she founded in 1933 and oversaw for nearly fifty years, was an effort to show that the radical Gospel commandment of love could be lived.

She understood this challenge not just in the personal form of charity (the works of mercy) but in a political form as well, confronting and resisting the social forces which gave rise to such a need for charity. She represented a new type of political holiness—a way of serving Christ not only through prayer and sacrifice, but through solidarity with the poor and in struggle along the path of justice and peace.

In some ways the seeds of her vocation lay in her childhood reflection on the saints. While she admired the sacrifice of saints who poured out their lives for the sick and poor and the victims of injustice, where, she asked herself, were the saints to *change* the social order, not just to minister to its victims? Disillusioned with the complacency of Christians, she turned instead to the radical movements of the day. Her friends were communists, socialists, and anarchists.

Eventually she returned to Christianity, but by an unusual route— particularly unusual in the annals of the saints. Specifically, she was inspired to become a Catholic after the birth of a daughter out of wedlock. Her joy at this experience was so great that it turned her heart to God. And yet this turning entailed great sacrifice. Her "common-law" husband was a committed atheist who would have nothing to do with marriage or religion. Her conversion entailed a separation from the man she loved, but at the same time a fear that in embracing the Church she was betraying the cause of the workers, of the poor.

After her conversion, she felt a great longing to find some way of reconciling her faith with her commitment to the poor and social justice. The Catholic Worker Movement, which she launched on May 1, 1933, represented the synthesis she had been seeking, a way of connecting "body and soul, this world and the next."[224]

Like many of the great saints, Day essentially invented her own path, different from the various alternatives available at the time. What is striking about her path is that, unlike the great founders of religious orders, she set out to launch this lay apostolic movement without seeking any support or authorization from Church authorities, daring to claim the name *Catholic* while staking out positions on war and peace and social justice that were far in advance of any conventional Church teaching of the time. By the time she died, she was widely regarded as the radical conscience of the American Catholic Church. In 2000, the Vatican accepted her cause for canonization, and she received the official title Servant of God.

Of all the women I have discussed, Dorothy Day is the only one I knew firsthand. I was privileged to work with her for the last five years of her life, and recently I edited her diaries, *The Duty of Delight*.[225] The greatest revelation in reading her diaries was to see how much her spirituality was worked out in the chores and duties of everyday life and in the constant struggle to practice love, patience, and forgiveness in her encounters with those around her.

The connection with Saint Thérèse was direct. (By coincidence, Day was born in the same year Thérèse died.) She wrote a book about Thérèse and frequently expressed her devotion to the Little Way. She particularly wished to develop the social implications of Thérèse's spirituality, emphasizing the potential power of all the little gestures we make—seemingly ineffective and marginal—in the case of peace and justice.

One tends to identify the saints with the great events in their lives. One's image of Dorothy Day, for instance, may focus on her imprisonment for civil disobedience, her fasting, and walking on picket lines. But most of her life was spent in very ordinary ways. Like Thérèse of Lisieux or Madeleine Delbrêl, she believed those ordinary events and duties were the place where she encountered God; they were the arena for heroism and the path to holiness.

Conclusions

What conclusions do I draw from the chronicles of women saints?

There are, of course, as many types of saints as there are people. Each saint offers a unique glimpse of the face of God; each enlarges our moral imagination; each offers new insights in the meaning and possibilities of human life. To the extent that women's names have been forgotten, their stories untold, their dreams, visions, and wisdom marginalized, these possibilities remain unknown and unfulfilled. We suffer the same loss when women's experience and examples are conformed to restrictive and stereotypical preconceptions of holiness.

But to hold up these lives is not just a matter of providing equal time. Because of the restrictions and obstacles they have overcome or transcended in a fundamentally patriarchal Church and culture, I find the example of women saints particularly compelling and inspiring. They dramatize in a special way the challenge we all face to discern our own way to holiness, apart from the well-worn paths of the past or the conventional wisdom of the present. So many women saints could share the motto applied to Saint Angela Merici, founder of the Ursuline order: "A Woman Faced with two Alternatives. She Saw and Chose the Third."[226]

Second, I find an inclusive, holistic spirituality at work in many women saints—less inclined to draw distinctions between the realm of the sacred and the profane; less inclined to indulge in abstraction; better prepared to recognize and embrace the sacred depths of everyday experience, whether of family, work, community, love, suffering, or the demands of ordinary life. The story of each holy person is also a story about God. Each story contains an invitation—not simply to imitate the good deeds of these women, but to enter into the larger universe they inhabited. What happens next is the beginning of our own story.

NOTES

204. *Blessed Among All Women: Women Saints, Prophets, and Witnesses for Our Time* (New York: Crossroad, 2005). This talk draws freely from the reflections in that book.

205. *All Saints: Daily Reflections on Saints, Prophets, and Witnesses for Our Time* (New York: Crossroad, 1997).

206. Kathleen Jones, *Women Saints* (Maryknoll, NY: Orbis Books, 1999), p. 242.

207. Penny Blaker Mitchell, *Mother Theodore Guerin: A Woman for Our Time* (Saint Mary-of-the-Woods, IN: Sisters of Providence, 1998), p. 54.

208. Ibid., p. 61.

209. Ibid., p. 67.

210. Ibid., p. 90.

211. Ibid., p. 100.

212. Kenneth L. Woodward, *Making Saints* (New York: Simon and Schuster, 1990), p. 276.

213. Juliana Wadham, *The Case of Cornelia Connelly* (New York: Pantheon, 1957), p. 160.

214. Ibid., p. 200.

215. Ibid., p. 300.

216. Ibid., p. 315.

217. *The Autobiography of St. Thérèse of Lisieux; The Story of a Soul* (New York: Doubleday, 1957), p. 153.

218. Ibid., p. 155.

219. Madeleine Delbrêl, *We, the Ordinary People of the Street*, trans. David Louis Schindler, Jr., and Charles F. Mann (Grand Rapids, MI: William B. Eerdmans, 2000), 54.

220. Ibid.

221. Ibid., p. 98.

222. Ibid., p. 58.

223. David O'Brien, "The Pilgrimage of Dorothy Day," *Commonweal*, December 1980.

224. Dorothy Day, *The Long Loneliness* (New York: Harper & Row, 1952), p. 151.

225. *The Duty of Delight: The Diaries of Dorothy Day*, ed. Robert Ellsberg (Milwaukee, WI: Marquette University Press, 2008).

226. I am grateful to Sister Dianna Ortiz, an Ursuline nun and the author of *The Blindfold's Eyes: My Journey from Torture to Truth*, for remembering this title from a life of St. Angela.

7. Which Mary, Which Woman, Which Church?

Mary Ann Zimmer, ND, PhD,
Assistant Professor of Religious Studies, Marywood University

Introduction

Considering the incredibly rich tradition of reflection on and devotion to Mary, it is necessary to be extremely selective for our purposes today. When we reflect on the influence of Mary of Nazareth, her impact on the Church has been so varied we really must ask, "Which Mary? Which woman? Which Church?"

Jesus spoke of the householder taking out from the family's store of treasure the new as well as the old (Matthew 14:52). Catholicism is continually carrying on such exploration around the tradition of Mary. We have in our Catholic storeroom some items that, though ancient, are obviously stunning jewels. We have some dusty treasures that will polish up amazingly well, some odd-shaped objects that puzzle us, some fascinating new or maybe familiar items that have been turned over and over and found revelatory from new angles. Some items have developed encrustations that can sharply pain a person who comes into contact with them.

In this short text, I am going to visit that storehouse with you. First, I will focus on two scriptural themes that have been a part of the Marian tradition from early days of Christianity: Mary's virginity and her role as disciple. Next, I will deal with a very early interpretation of Mary as the new Eve. Two of these early themes, virginity and the new Eve, have influenced the Christian tradition in a direction particularly ambiguous if not damaging for women. Finally, I will propose some places where all of us might contribute to the Church's history of continually unfolding and developing our understanding of the Mary who can still accompany, challenge, and inspire us today.

To set the scene, however, I encourage you to begin by considering a few images of Mary.

Images of Mary

Because the portrayal of Mary in arts of every kind is so telling, it is instructive to begin by considering her representation at various points in history. Fortunately, the Internet makes it possible at least to sample the wide variety of such images.

The first is *The Intercession of Christ and the Virgin,* an early fifteenth-century painting by Lorenzo Monaco found at the Cloisters Museum[227] in New York. The picture contains a trinity of large figures arranged in a triangle, with God the Father in heaven at the apex, Christ at the left, and the Virgin at the right. Mary and Christ are interceding with their expressions and gestures for a small group of smaller figures kneeling in front of Mary facing Christ. The smallest figure is a dove, which represents the Holy Spirit, flying from the Father to Christ and completing the official Trinity. The question this painting raises is the identity of the *functional* Trinity for the artist and those who viewed the picture.

The second image is an illumination from the Rohan Master's *Book of Hours,* also from the early fifteenth century. Called the *Flight into Egypt, Grain Miracle,* it can be found on the cover of *The Goddess Obscured* by Pamela Berger. It depicts the Holy Family being pursued by soldiers who pause to speak to a peasant reaping grain. The miracle is that the peasant was sowing when the Holy Family passed by, but his wheat has miraculously sprouted and ripened. He can truthfully follow Mary's command to tell the soldiers that he did see the fleeing family, but it was when he was sowing his grain.

Berger traces the way a story of the miraculous growth of grain associated with a pre-Christian grain goddess mutates into a devotion to various saints, in this case, the Virgin Mary. She argues that peasant life was so precarious and their crops so vital that, even with the introduction of Christianity, farmers could not trust their survival without continuing the rites that protected their harvests. Church officials opposed these rituals, but the peasants simply carried them on in various disguised or transmuted forms. What we see here is a case in which Mary carries out a divine function when the official God is represented as detached from deeply felt needs.[228]

The final three images are contemporary. Yolanda López has painted several well-known versions of Our Lady of Guadalupe.[229] The most famous is Mary as a jogging self-portrait of the artist. She is striding out with great energy and carrying Mary's blue and gold cloak behind her like a banner. The series includes portraits of her plump mother at her sewing machine, her elderly grandmother, and the Goddess Coatilcue—all as Guadalupes. López portrays the sacred not as distant, meek, physically perfect, unattainable, or under the control of the Church, but as immediately present in the ordinary lives of women.[230]

A second contemporary image is the very pregnant Mary who graces the pages of Julie Vivas's illustrations in the children's book *Nativity.*[231] This is the most pregnant Mary possible, and she and Joseph face the daunting task of getting her on a donkey. I cannot recommend it highly enough for a humanizing look at Mary's reality. The wise men find Mary at the house with all the diapers on the clothesline. Vivas's beautiful watercolors raise questions about why there is so little artwork portraying Mary as pregnant or her family as ordinary.

The third contemporary image is more elusive. In a search for a sense of Mary as realistically Middle Eastern, one can find some photos of contemporary Palestinian mothers and children.[232] The single image I could find in art is by Palestinian artist Ismail Shammout, who portrays her as the *Bethlehem Virgin*.[233]

What do these images say to us? Are any of them closer to Mary's reality than conventional madonnas? Why is this heritage so neglected?

Our imaginations awakened, we turn now to the texts in the storehouse of Marian tradition. We begin with Scripture.

Mary in Scripture: Two Considerations

Some of the ways Mary appears in Scripture are as 1) a recipient of God's favor; 2) a woman willing to consent to a very unusual proposal from God; 3) the loving, agonized parent of Jesus; 4) the mother of an executed prisoner; and 5) a disciple of Jesus' way. Much has been written about each of these; for our purposes, I will focus on two: Mary's *virginity*, an issue that arises from the annunciation account, and her *discipleship* and its connection with her *agonized motherhood*.

Mary in Her Virginity

This aspect of the Marian tradition reminds me of a puzzle cube with a clear and mostly positive picture on each side. Unfortunately, as most of us have known them, these pictures have been scrambled, sometimes with sad or painful results.

The issue of Mary's virginity arises in the infancy narratives of Matthew's and Luke's Gospels. Matthew's Gospel focuses on Joseph as the active figure. He struggles over Mary's becoming pregnant before the two, though betrothed, have come to live together. An angel in a dream reassures him that "the child conceived in her is from the Holy Spirit" (Matthew 1:18–23). In the infancy narrative of Luke, it is Mary who, though frightened and unmarried, gives her consent to the overshadowing of the Holy Spirit that will make her the mother of a son to whom God promises to give the throne of David (Luke 1:32).[234]

In the Gospels, the focus of these incidents is the power of God's Holy Spirit, to give life. The story of Jesus' conception had well-known precedents in the Hebrew Scriptures in the form of the conception of special children who were born of parents whose inability to conceive was unambiguously described. Their well-established barrenness made it clear that Sarah (Gen 18:11), Samson's mother (Judges 13:2), Hannah, the mother of Samuel, (1 Samuel 1:19), and Elizabeth (Luke 1:7) were *only* pregnant through the power of God.[235] Mary, too, was to bear a child through the power of the Holy Spirit. In this case, God's will and power are more sharply emphasized by Mary's conceiving, not in spite of age or of proven barrenness, but outside of any sexual relationship. Thus Jesus' conception, through intervention by God, parallels that of certain Old Testament figures and of John the Baptist.

At the same time, Jesus is clearly set off as an exceptional figure. This exceptional and salvific work of God is a beautiful picture on one side of our cube. Mary's assent (a different quality, I would argue, than obedience) is another.

Given later developments in attitudes toward sexuality, it is important to affirm that there is no place in these Gospel accounts themselves for the attitude that forgoing sexual activity might be a more "pure" way to achieve God's purposes. To the first-century Israelite, it was clear from Genesis that God created humanity male and female, pronounced this creation "good," and told them to cleave to one another and to be fruitful.[236] At the same time, as Mary Foskett points out, readers develop their understanding of a character using both the information given in the text and the culturally available material of their own times, forming a complex, composite character that goes beyond the text and will differ in different cultural contexts.[237]

What did the early-Church preachers and theologians make of these passages? Very early on, the focus was not on devotion to Mary as such. Early writers used the accounts of Jesus' conception to defend their belief in Jesus' full humanity against those who would try to minimize or deny it. Ignatius of Antioch in the early second century described Jesus as unique having "sprung from Mary and from God."[238] Later, the proper understanding of Mary's titles would come to the fore in a different set of debates, those that struggled to express that Jesus is one reality with two radically different natures—divine and human. The affirmation at the Council of Ephesus (431) that Mary could properly be called *Theotokos* (God-bearing) was meant to confirm the view that neither the humanity nor the divinity of Christ could be divided from his total unity. These affirmations form another two sides of our cube.

Eventually, Mary's virginal state came to be a topic of reflection in itself.

This fact must be understood, however, within an extremely complex set of religious meanings and motivations driving Greco-Roman and Christian practices of self-denial and self-discipline in the early centuries of Christianity. This topic could be an entire box of puzzle cubes in itself. The picture is so rich and varied that a whole body of literature is required to attempt to describe it. If one reads early Christian literature today without a sense of its complex environment, it can seem simply antibody and/or antisexuality, and in some cases antiwoman. No doubt there have been such strands. At the same time, a complex literature taken out of context has also been used to perpetuate such views.

A further complication is that such ancient points of view come to us only from those who had the education, status, security, and leisure to teach and write. We will know little or nothing about the lives of more ordinary people, the marginal, or most women. What we do know about women will come to us only from the viewpoint of men. What we read is also the ideal, what people should do or the proscribed, what they should not be doing. It does not tell us how they actually lived.

Peter Brown describes the complex landscape within which Christians made ascetic choices. It is only possible to sample it here. In the context of the Roman Empire, for example, reproduction was a civic duty. Citizens were expected to reproduce to replenish the population. In this context, some groups of Christians chose to abstain from sexual relations as a way to resist the civic duty to reproduce, thus hastening the end of the present time and helping to ushering in the final age initiated by Jesus' resurrection.[239]

Another viewpoint is represented by groups such as that led by the teacher Valentinus (died 165). His followers' dualistic world view regarded the creation of the material world and the soul as a mistake. This mistake would be rectified through a baptism that would unite the positive elements of the self, the spirit, with its own guardian angel and bring into one all divisions of body/soul/spirit and male/female. In this system, the finally redeemed would be free of all sexual desire—and would be essentially male.[240] Valentinus' followers would only gradually, over time, come to be considered outside the mainstream Christian understanding.

Another prominent influence was *stoicism*, a philosophical world view widespread in the empire. This system of philosophy valued serene, reasoned responses to all life situations and considered the passions an obstacle to that life. Brown, in his reading of the stoics, differentiates the passions and the emotions. The passions can be described as inner forces that could cause an intemperate response—positive or negative—to one or another situation.

This did not preclude enjoyment of sexuality and its unitive effect in marriage, but this was to be measured and directed toward its reasonable end: procreation. In some settings, Christians called attention to their admirable, or even superior, mode of life by going the stoics one better and refraining from all sexual activity. Others like Clement of Alexandria (died circa 215), who was married, defended the good of marriage with an attitude that would be recognizable to the stoics. Brown points out, however, that Clement, unlike the stoics, had no place for a unitive effect of sexual pleasure, a lack Brown finds definitive for future Christian views of marriage.[241]

In early Christianity, a life of asceticism might have been built around virginity, continence in marriage, or a decision not to remarry after widowhood. Of these possibilities, virginity came to have pride of place. This was particularly true as the fifth century reached its midpoint. Augustine (died 430), for example, says to Juliana, a devout widow married only once, that her virgin daughter "coming after you in birth, has gone before you in conduct."[242]

At this period, devotion to Mary as virgin came to the fore. Devout Christians identified with her humanity but honored it as more perfect than their own. She was free from the processes of intercourse and normal birth that signaled to the average Christian that their bodies were fallen and uncontrollable.[243]

In its Gospel context, Mary's virginity was a sign of the life-giving power of God. Now it had shifted to being a sign of a superior and unattainable asexual purity that is most closely approximated by a life of consecrated virginity. This ideal, however, casts a shadow over women such that all other women live under a cloud that hovers over all sexuality, even within committed marriage. If Mary is, as one song in our missalette has it "virgin mother undefiled," how are all other mothers to be understood?

The most unfortunate aspect of this attitude has been the second-class spiritual status long felt by married women and men in the Church. A second aspect I grieve is the way it can turn the lives of married women and women religious into a competition rather than a rich source of mutual inspiration and support. Finally, it has at many points generated an antibody attitude that separates Christians from God's good creation as well as from a full realization of the wonder of the Incarnation.

Elizabeth Johnson has pointed out that there are other ways we idealize Mary and separate her from the human reality of the rest of us. One way is through the assumption that her discipleship was immediate, untroubled, and automatic.

Mary As Agonized Mother and Disciple

The cool, serene beauty of the traditional Madonna figure has its theological theme: trust in God's grace is the primary force in her life, bestowing peace and beauty. This does not mean we should let ourselves turn that theological affirmation into a damaging distance that separates her—and Jesus—from our lives. It is precisely to lead us into shared Communion that God's grace acts. Our understanding of Mary's concrete, conflicted human situation has been greatly enhanced by recent use of anthropological information by Scripture scholars. This helps us flesh out our understanding of the lives of Jesus, Mary, and Joseph and to put the Gospel message into context.

It also helps us connect it to real life today. It rescues Mary from the frequent portrayal of her and her family as always clean, tranquil, and sweat-free, speaking to one another only in polite, modulated voices, and untouched by any of the upheaval that frequently visits real human life. In her amazing book, *Truly Our Sister*, Elizabeth Johnson brings Mary's life into focus as a person like us, available to accompany us in our struggles rather than looking on from a distant pedestal. From this point of view, Mary can be seen as a loving but struggling parent. It is this parent rather than some perfect, unquestioning Mary whose discipleship we will consider.

Elizabeth Johnson describes first-century Nazareth as a village of poor farmers and the artisans who served their needs—all living a hand-to-mouth existence without economic security or cushion. They lived as people of an occupied land who were taxed into desperation by temple, King Herod, and Rome. They lived in constant threat from uprisings and the occupying army's brutal response. In 4 BCE, for example, two thousand Jewish men were crucified in the suppression of a rebellion. Needless to say, this setting was a time and place in which it would be extremely dangerous to go about proclaiming the inbreaking and final triumph of the kingdom of God.[244]

Knowing this social history helps us realize the plain, practical wisdom of Jesus' mother and other family members in their initial reaction to his mission of proclaiming God's kingdom. The earliest of these accounts appears in Mark (3:20–21, 31–35). As a crowd, so large that Jesus and the disciples could not even eat, gathers around Jesus, his family "went out to restrain him, for people were saying 'He has gone out of his mind.'" Given the volatile and repressive political situation, it makes perfect sense that those who cared most about him would try to protect him from the real and dire consequences of his behavior. When Jesus hears that "his mother and brothers" are asking for him, he says, "'Who are my mother and my brothers?' And looking at those who sat around him, he said, 'Here are my mother and my brothers! Whoever does the will of God is my brother and sister and mothers.'" This response performs a shocking replacement of the "natural" family with a new set of relationships that belongs to those committed to God's will as it is expressed in Jesus' message.

The later Gospels omit the embarrassing aspects of the family's mission. They also soften (Matthew 12:46–50) or omit (Luke 8:19–20) this radical contrast Jesus makes. In this configuration, Mary's understanding of Jesus does not seem so problematic.[245]

Mary's eventual understanding and acceptance of Jesus' mission, her discipleship, is clearly portrayed by Luke when he names her as present after the ascension in the upper room where the Pentecost experience would take place. She is described as being there with the apostles, a number of other women, and Jesus' brothers, who "were constantly devoting themselves to prayer" (Acts 1:12–14). Elizabeth Johnson maintains that Mary's attempt to intervene in Jesus' predictable fate was not due to a lack of faith but an expression of her faith that God wants life to be preserved. This faith has been shared by women everywhere who have held onto and acted on that conviction when faced with danger to their loved ones. When we acknowledge that, we can see that Mary's faithfulness to God is consistent and her commitment to discipleship in Jesus' way is at least as hard won as our own.[246]

When we consider the tradition, we see a constant interplay between those beliefs and images that bring Mary into the human realm with us and those that separate and distance her. The new Eve is one of those distancing images.

Mary As the New Eve

The interpretation of Mary as the "new Eve" is a very early image in the writings of the Christian preachers and theologians and one that has persisted. It is not explicitly scriptural but probably parallels Paul's comparison of Adam to Jesus, the new Adam: "for as all die in Adam, so all will be made alive in Christ" and "'the first man, Adam, became a living being'; the last Adam becomes a life-giving spirit" (1 Corinthians 15:22, 45). The image of Mary as the new Eve appears in the Dogmatic Constitution on the Church (*Lumen Gentium*) of Vatican II in its chapter on Mary. In the words of Irenaeus in the second century, "the knot of Eve's disobedience was untied by Mary's obedience: what the virgin Eve bound through her disbelief, Mary loosened by her faith." In the same paragraph we find the fourth-century expression by Jerome: "death through Eve, life through Mary."[247]

The unfortunate reality is that the positive evaluation of the woman, Mary, in this image has not functioned to elevate women as a whole from being identified as temptresses or as the original "Eve" still endangering their human companions. Women in general continued to be identified with sinful Eve, while Mary became the contrast or exception to all other females. As Elizabeth Johnson points out, this form of idealization continues to permit the veneration of the heavenly Mary while excusing the control and domination of actual contemporary women.[248]

Contemporary Challenges

How might actual contemporary women and men claim their own images and traditions around Mary?

I propose four possibilities for our own era in relationship to Mary. I offer them for your consideration as gifts God might be offering us, gifts we might develop for one another and our Church.

1. Solidarity with Mary of the at-risk pregnancy in the at-risk life

Mary calls us to solidarity with the humanity of the oppressed world as our shared humanity. As Elizabeth Johnson so eloquently describes the situation, this is our sister. When we consider her as fully human rather than semidivine, she draws us into the broader human condition of all those in dire straits. Mary found herself endangered by an illicit pregnancy and bearing a vulnerable child into an economically and politically precarious situation.[249] This is the locus of God's visitation and commitment. How does it become ours?

One of the ways this can happen for us today is for us to embrace the grace of global solidarity. It is common to talk about the need for solidarity with the oppressed. It is important to be clear that this is not about making solidarity happen, but about the choice of opening ourselves to an inescapable solidarity that already exists. We are only too slowly becoming aware that one cannot simply throw trash "away" because there is no "away," no magic land into which our refuse can disappear. In the same vein, we are one humanity; our lives impact each other whether we choose to take cognizance of that or responsibility for it. We can construct a pseudoisolation, like children who believe that they disappear just because they have their eyes shut. There is no similar process to make ourselves and our needs the only ones on the planet.

Why would God call Christians to a life of solidarity with the vulnerable? It is not for the purpose of some cruel program to increase their sense of guilt or hopelessness or so that everyone's stress levels will intensify. God calls

Christians to live in solidarity because this is the richest vision of humanity one can embrace. This is the graced location for being met by God. Mary proclaims this vision in her Magnificat—the perfect prayer to accompany, inspire, and support this effort.

2. The Maryam shared with Islam

The Mary Christians think of as "belonging" to them is honored as *Maryam* in the Koran in chapter 19, which is named for her. Her life is described in a text that focuses on her preparation by God to become the virgin mother of the great prophet Jesus. Maryam is honored particularly in the mystical expressions of Islam.[250] My Muslim students are often eager for Christians to understand the respect they extend to both Mary and Jesus who, while clearly not divine, is honored as a major prophet. They believe, correctly I think, that this information would be at least a small step in mending the ignorance and prejudiced attitudes that have grown up around Islam in this country. What would it mean for Christians to ask for instruction in the Muslim understanding of this Maryam and her role in the Koran and in Muslim piety? What fruit might this yield as a small but concrete step for peace and interfaith understanding?

3. The Virgin of Guadalupe, Patroness of (all) the Americas

In 1946 Pope Pius XII declared Our Lady of Guadalupe the patroness of the Americas. Despite this, her role in the U.S. Catholic Church is largely limited to the Spanish-speaking population or people of Mexican heritage. What would it mean for Anglo Catholics to take up this patronage in a serious way? Can we see ourselves as *one* of the Americas? Can we recognize the beauty, instruction, and grace coming to us from something we did not invent, we do not control, we did not see first, we did not name, and we cannot buy? How do we let Mary's patronage call us to the common good of the Americas that do not belong to us alone?

4. Attention to the unsanctioned Mary as companion in Christian life

What I mean by the unsanctioned Mary is the multifaceted Mary who operates in the lives of the ordinary baptized Christian. Historically, this Mary has not always been a handmaid of current fashions in official doctrine or practice. Apparitions and devotions are not always immediately endorsed. Respect for one's own religious experience, however, is one way to be attentive to grace, and so is a gift to the Church. I do not mean to romanticize this. As Paul says, all spirits need to be tested, and clearly not all religious experience is positive. At the same time, the Holy Spirit is a gift of baptism and exercises its power without asking anyone's permission. We will never know what the Spirit is currently saying to us unless we risk receiving and sharing what we hear.

The unsanctioned Mary often appears to and speaks with the marginal. She keeps reappearing in piety to attend to the concerns that the God of the institution does not have time for. We see this, for example, in the "grain goddess" tradition. Was the transfer of planting and harvest rituals to Mary's patronage an example of heresy, an unfortunate syncretism, or a witness to God's very real concern for mundane anxieties and a critique of the "official God"? The images, stories, and devotions of the ages have constantly brought God back to the material world and the daily struggle to live in that world.

One way to be in solidarity with the unsanctioned Mary is to take responsibility for our images. As Paul Ricoeur instructs, we do not necessarily have thoughts and choose to express them in symbols. Rather "the symbol gives rise to thought."[251] The images we choose to populate our imagination can control what we think it is possible for God to be concerned about, to honor, to do. This is particularly important when it comes to Mary because of her connection in Christian thought with the reality of Jesus' own humanity. With this in mind, do we have only images of Mary that are slender, caucasian, conventionally pretty by U.S. standards of the twenty-first century? Is she ever very pregnant? Overweight? Aged? Is she in any way realistically Middle Eastern? How is she dressed? Do the images we create, accept, demand, and use lead us toward or away from human solidarity? Will her role continue to gravitate toward divine rather than human qualities as long as the symbolism of the institutional Church continues to insist on images of God that are controlled by a hierarchical, celibate, male power structure?

God continues to call our attention to the really real. We are to respect that call as it comes to us.

Conclusion

After looking closely at only a few of the items in the storeroom of Marian tradition, you may feel some items should be approached with caution or kept on a back shelf. Some help us stay in touch with the concrete reality of the Incarnation. Some call us to affirm the dignity of women and to awaken to solidarity with the marginalized. Others invite us to enter into alliance with Mary to trust in our own experience of God and in God's sometimes unlikely will for God's people.

NOTES

227. Search the Cloisters Museum Web site at www.metmuseum.org/Works_Of_Art/the_cloisters.

228. Pamela Berger, *The Goddess Obscured: Transformation of the Grain Protectress From Goddess to Saint* (Boston: Beacon Press, 2001). An Internet search of the title will show this work on the cover of the book.

229. See International Marian Research Institute, (University of Dayton, http://campus.udayton.edu/mary//gallery/exhibits/chicana/works.html).

230. Elinor W. Gadon, *The Once and Future Goddess: A Symbol for Our Time* (San Francisco: Harper & Row, 1989), fig. 48.

231. Julie Vivas, illus., *Nativity* (Voyager, 1986). An Internet search of the illustrator will show a sample of her work on the cover of the book.

232. See www.daylife.com/photo/08Gt3Fe62f1ux and www.jamd.com/image/g/51103518.

233. www.palestineonlinestore.com/art/tamam.html.

234. The definitive commentary on these texts is Raymond E. Brown, *The Birth of the Messiah: A Commentary on the Infancy Narrative in Matthew and Luke.* (Garden City, New York: Image Books, 1979).

235. Raymond E. Brown, et al., *Mary in the New Testament* (Philadelphia: Fortress, 1978), 112–13.

236. Writings found at Qumran confirm that a celibate community was formed there, but this was definitely not the mainstream first-century practice. That said, contemporary scholars are finding added complexity to the picture of asceticism in first-century Judaism. See the discussion in Elizabeth A. Clark, *Reading Renunciation: Asceticism and Scripture in Early Christianity* (Princeton: Princeton University Press, 1999), 21–22.

237. Mary F. Foskett, *A Virgin Conceived: Mary and Classical Representations of Virginity* (Bloomington, IN: Indiana University Press, 2002), 4.

238. Quoted in Tina Beattie, "Mary in Patristic Theology," in *Mary: The Complete Resource*, ed. Sarah Jane Boss (New York: Oxford University Press, 2007), 82–83.

239. Peter Brown, *The Body and Society: Men, Women and Sexual Renunciation in Early Christianity*, Lectures on the History of Religions, vol. 13 (New York: Columbia University Press, 1988), 307.

240. Peter Brown, *Body and Society*, 103–21.

241. Peter Brown, *Body and Society*, 179–33.

242. Quoted in Gillian Cloke, *This Female Man of God: Women and Spiritual Power in the Patristic Age* (London: Routledge, 1995), 58.

243. Peter Brown, *Body and Society*, 444.

244. Elizabeth A. Johnson, *Truly Our Sister: A Theology of Mary in the Communion of Saints* (New York: Continuum, 2003), 137–61. For a shorter treatment, see *Dangerous Memories: A Mosaic of Mary in Scripture (Continuum, 2004)*. This volume contains the chapters from *Truly Our Sister* that focus on Mary in Scripture.

245. Johnson, *Truly Our Sister*, 217–19.

246. Johnson, *Truly Our Sister*, 221.

247. Dogmatic Constitution on the Church, #56. In: Flannery, Austin, O.P., *Vatican II: The Conciliar and Post Conciliar Documents*, New Revised Edition (Northport, NY: Costello Publishing).

248. Johnson, *Truly Our Sister*, 23–25.

249. Johnson, *Truly Our Sister*, 226–40.

250. See Tim Winter, "Mary in Islam," in *Mary: The Complete Resource*, ed. Sarah Jane Boss (New York: Oxford University Press, 2007), 479–502 and N. J. Dawood, trans., *The Koran* (London: Penguin Books, 2003).

251. Paul Ricoeur, *The Symbolism of Evil*, trans. Emerson Buchanan (Boston: Beacon Press, 1969), 347–57. For a clear exposition of this point see Elizabeth Johnson, *She Who Is: The Mystery of God in Feminist Theological Discourse*, (New York: Crossroad, 1994), 47.

Panel Discussion

Moderator: Richard W. Miller

Panel: Eileen Burke-Sullivan
Susan Calef
William Harmless
Gary Macy
Mary Ann Zimmer

Richard Miller: The first question is for Dr. Calef. Why was Mary Magdalene considered a whore? What was the history that led to that? Could you describe that?

Susan Calef: Mary Magdalene—how did she become a whore? Well, it's a long story. Actually, dear old Dan Brown, my friend Dan Brown, in his beloved book claims (he has this salacious taste for conspiracies, as you know), it is the legacy of the smear campaign, to cover up that she was the Holy Grail, which is, quite frankly, nonsense.

It really goes back to a misreading of the biblical texts. First of all, there is kind of a muddle of Marys. There are numerous Marys in the New Testament; Mary would have been a very common name for women at the time of Jesus, so you've got that problem. Mary Magdalene gets confused in the reading of the text with a couple of other Marys, like Mary of Bethany (the Mary of the Mary-and-Martha sisterhood), and then also some anonymous women who are not named in the Gospels, like the unnamed woman, the so-called sinful woman of Luke 7, who is anointing Jesus' feet with her tears and wiping his feet with her hair. This very sensual scene includes an anonymous woman. She is not named. It is not Mary Magdalene in the opinion of most scholars. So you've got that scene.

You've also got, then, later in John's Gospel, that anointing scene where the woman gets named Mary; it's not Mary of Magdalene, it is Mary of the Mary-and-Martha team or sisterhood. So, what really happens is, of course in Luke 7, the story of the "sinful woman," that gets interpreted as a sexual sin, even though that is not clear in the text and different arguments are made by scholars as to whether we should assume her sin is sexual. In any case, that's where you get that link with sexuality, sensuality, sexual sin.

Then, of course, you've also got the anonymous woman in John's Gospel, the so-called adulterous woman who is never named. So what happens is, very early on, it starts to show up in the early centuries, you start seeing all this conflation of the different Marys as well as these anonymous women. Once you hit Gregory the Great in the sixth century, he gives a sermon where he really talks about and makes quite clear that he feels Mary Magdalene is indeed that woman from Luke 7 and so forth. He launches into, and I'll just read you a little piece of this: "She whom Luke calls the sinful woman whom John calls Mary, we believe to be the Mary from whom seven devils were ejected." In other words, Mary Magdalene. And then he goes on to link those seven devils with the Seven Deadly Sins, including lust and all that other. So from then on in the tradition, that really takes off. But I certainly would not see it the way Dan Brown does, that somehow Gregory had this malevolent intent in doing that. It is a very regrettable misreading of the biblical texts.

Richard Miller: The second question is for Dr. Calef and Dr. Harmless. When did the various ministries become more male dominant? Or how and when did the relative equality in the first hundred years become *more* male dominated?

Susan Calef: With regard to the Pauline communities, the ministry in those communities that early seems to have been very charismatic. It was about people having received certain spiritual gifts. For example, that's why in 1 Corinthians 11:2–16, it is clear that women were prophesying in the assembly; women were prophets. And Paul doesn't have any issues with that; he just wants their heads covered. So early on there is a certain kind of egalitarianism. It is not really an appropriate word for it; that was certainly not their mentality at that time, and it is anachronistic to speak of it that way. But certainly men and women were working together in the Pauline communities. You already start to see some change in the New Testament. If you read the later Pauline material (the pastorals, the other Deutero-Pauline texts), you begin to see an effort arising to try to put women back in another place. So pretty quickly, right in the New Testament evidence, you will see a struggle, and that struggle over women's place will continue from then on up to today.

William Harmless: On a factual level, my impression is that the Church has always been male dominated, the question is the degree of latitude and range of women's participation in a variety of ministries in a variety of ways. And that has certain ups and downs. So I would not tend to see it as an equality even in the New Testament. But there are certainly more porous or more fluid patterns. But there is always a level of counter-protest movements. There is a strong women's movement in a bit of a harebrained prophetic movement called the Montanus in the late second century, and while it was led by a man, two very remarkable and unusual women were prophetesses within that context. But one of the things I tried to point out is the variety of ministries of women that we tend not to pay attention to. If we simply look at official functions, there are a whole lot of other very important things going on for which the very life of the Church was at stake, and it was often those women benefactors, the Olympiases, the Melanias the Elder, who really had key roles in bankrolling the Church, and we could never underestimate the significance of that.

Susan Calef: One additional thing. At times you hear the phrase, with regard to the Jesus Movement, "the discipleship of equals." And that phrase comes particularly out of Elisabeth Schüssler-Fiorenza. As much as I respect Elisabeth's work and am grateful for much of what she's done to blaze the trail in feminist biblical interpretation, I don't agree with her on that. I don't think we should think of Jesus' movement in that way. It was the reign-of-God movement, and gender per se was not on the screen. He certainly accepted women into his entourage; as I said earlier today, I think Mary Magdalene was a very important member of that group and may have even had a special friendship with Jesus. Who knows? But I think at times her work has given people the impression that somehow Jesus was a kind of protofeminist who was deliberately trying to advance the cause of women. I don't think that was on the screen. I think much of what he was about in the reign-of-God movement obviously was attractive to women and drew people in; the way he operated, obviously, was very attractive to women. So I don't like that term "discipleship of equals," particularly when we are trying to talk historically about what it was really like.

Richard Miller: Dr. Harmless, this would be again for you. Can you speak to Paula's role in Jerome's *Vulgate* project?

William Harmless: Jerome's *Vulgate* project was very important. Most fourth-century Latin-speaking Christians read what is called the *Vetus Latina* ("Old Latin"), and there were a number of versions of it, just as in your average bookstore today we have multiple English translations of varying qualities. The majority of these early Latin translations were really awful. Jerome set about to try to do a more scholarly translation in more elegant Latin. His version better reflected the original Greek New Testament and the original Hebrew Old Testament. His choice of translating directly from the Hebrew was very controversial at the time, as one sees in the correspondence between him and Saint Augustine. By the way, we call him *Saint* Jerome. Well, if *he's* a saint, we've all got a shot! Jerome was one of the great curmudgeons in the history of Christianity. He may have been a great scholar but, boy, you did not want to be on his bad side. He blackened the reputation of Melania the Elder. He waged a very bitter personal vendetta against her and against Rufinus. So it is neither *Saint* Rufinus nor *Saint* Melania, where by any other standards they both would have been canonized.

Initially, I heard you ask not about "Paula," but about "Paul." One of Jerome's early projects was writing verse-by-verse commentaries on Paul's letters. These have yet to be translated into English. I've read only a section of them, mainly because I'm in the process of sorting out a point of controversy between him and Augustine.

As regards Paula's role in Jerome's *Vulgate* project, Paula was for Jerome what Melania was for Rufinus: a wealthy woman who underwrote his (expensive) intellectual project there in the Holy Land, a key day-to-day intellectual conversation partner and, of course, simply a very good friend. Paula and Jerome settled in Bethlehem, whereas Melania and Rufinus had settled just outside Jerusalem on the Mount of Olives. I'm not sure about how directly Paula influenced Jerome's *Vulgate* project—especially his turn to what he called "Hebrew verity," that is, reading the Old Testament in the original Hebrew and translating from that. She was certainly very interested in his biblical scholarship. She apparently was much taken with allegorical interpretation. It was at Paula's request that he translated Origen's *Homilies on Luke*. But, of course, Jerome made a very abrupt about-face on Origen— and Origen was the highly contentious issue between him and Rufinus (and thus Melania). Jerome did dedicate a number of his biblical projects to Paula, whom he speaks of in his prefaces. His early translation of the psalms was at her request. Paula headed the women's convent in Bethlehem until her death in 404. For more on Paula, I recommend reading J. N. D. Kelly's classic biography of Jerome.

Richard Miller: Dr. Harmless and Dr. Macy, what is going on when we talk about the abbesses hearing confessions? Please speak to this issue of hearing confessions in the early Church and the medieval Church.

William Harmless: I'll do the early Church. This may surprise contemporary Catholics, but when I hear the talk about hearing confessions, I do not think of that, in that period, as a priestly ministry. In the penance in the public episcopal churches—that is, churches run by bishops, which was the average church in the ancient world—the one form of penance was public penance. You got to do it once in your life, and it was for a major sin: murder, adultery, apostasy. The Desert Fathers in Egypt started developing this unique pattern of what we would now think of as private confession or spiritual direction. You would go to your *Abba*, the spiritual master, probably once a week, certainly any time you were troubled, and reveal to him your thoughts. And the gift of the *Abba* was to read your heart. So you would say good things and bad things and the ambiguous things. You would say things like, "Maybe I should leave the desert and go back to my home and convert my family to Christianity. Is that a good thing, or is that a temptation?" So it would be what we call the discernment of spirits, and your *Abba* would say, "No, I think you're being tempted to abandon your commitments." That is a monastic tradition.

In the Greek Orthodox Church, you probably would not got to a priest for confession; you would go to a monk. And so in the Greek Orthodox tradition, hearing confessions is not associated as a necessarily priestly thing. Now, you might have a bishop who is an ex-monk and is seen as holy, but you go to holy people to have your confession. One of the things that Gary would obviously study is a process of things you might call the monasticization of the clergy; that is, things that in the period I study I associate with monks who may or may not be clergy then become the norm for all clergy and are actually more patterns of monasticism. One of the things you also have to realize is that in the early medieval period, a lot of the evangelists who re-Christianized Europe after the Barbarians sort of de-Christianized Europe were Irish monks, and they bring their monastic traditions with them.

Gary Macy: The Irish and the Anglo-Saxon monks, because many of the Anglo-Saxons were trained originally in Irish schools and monasteries and then started their own schools and monasteries, re-Christianized Europe. There is a slow movement from confession being public penance to confession being basically spiritual direction, where you would go to your abbot or your abbess rather than your parish priest to confess your sins or to discuss your spiritual life. Public penance is still there, but slowly, slowly, slowly, this kind of spiritual direction becomes a more formal kind of sacramental confession.

And it's not altogether clear who you can confess to. You can go to a holy person, probably the big changing point there is the twelfth into the thirteenth century again. A huge change takes place in the structure of Christianity in the eleventh century reform movement which gets played out in the twelfth century. These reforms never take a short bit of time. And that's probably the structure we have inherited, the one that comes out of the thirteenth century. And it is not until the end of the thirteenth century that it's clear that you could only confess and be forgiven by a priest, so it would make perfect sense to go to an abbess if she was the one who was in charge of your area and she was the holy person.

Not all of the missionaries, by the way, were men. When Saint Boniface went out, he went with one of his close relatives, a very well-educated woman, and they were missionaries out there together. But again, that's a story that's only partly told. So men and women were doing that, and as abbesses and abbots they would both hear confessions. You wouldn't go necessarily to a priest. But that changes in the eleventh century in what is called the Grego rian Reform Movement.

Eileen Burke-Sullivan: Can I just throw in one thing on that too? The Roman leadership really fought against the private auricular confession for almost 400 years, forbade it at a number of councils, saw it as dangerous work and forbade it in all kinds of ways. When it finally was accepted, it was like overnight, more or less, and the Church said, "As we have consistently always taught, this is the practice that we will now carry forward." Also, the soldiers in the Crusades confessed to one another before they went into battle, and that was kind of a breaking point, I think.

Gary Macy: It's all during that same time period There was a fantastic change in Western civilization in the eleventh and twelfth centuries to create the world that we have now. It's a great story.

Richard Miller: Dr. Harmless and Dr. Macy, and Dr. Calef, you could jump in here if you'd like: what is a priest? How is *presbytera* understood in the early Church and how is it understood in the Middle Ages?

William Harmless: If you are a pagan or a Jew and you heard the word *priest*, you would presume animal sacrifice. Christians don't do animal sacrifice, so Christian clergy were not called priests for a long time. The term *priest* begins to be applied to Christian clergy only around the early 200s by Origen. One of the issues there is what do you do with the Old Testament?

Some groups were saying, "No, we just go with the New Testament, not the Old Testament." And Origen, one of the key people, will say, "No, the Old Testament is Scripture." He says it provides a foreshadowing of the New Testament. So while the Christian clergy don't do animal sacrifice, they do a sacrifice of the spirit.

So Origen begins applying the word *priest* to bishops. Remember, the order in the early Church is basically the bishop on top, a single bishop. In your average Roman town, you have a single bishop and you have one Church, and the bishop is the pastor of it, and then he has elders (presbyters) as advisors and who probably cover the Eucharist when he is away. Then you have the deacons, who handle what we would call social ministries. So you have both in the Greek East with Origen and then with Cyprian in the Latin West, the language of *priest* applied to the Christian clergy for the first time and almost exclusively to bishops. In the Latin West with Saint Augustine around the year 400 and in the Greek East, right around the year 400 by Saint John Chrysostom, they start pushing it and start applying the language of priesthood to presbyters.

And so, one of the issues Gary and I were talking about with his book, and he was struggling—how do I translate…? I am working on translating Augustine. When I see the word *presbyterus*, I just translate it as "presbyter," "an elder." And it's not the same word as *sacerdos*, which is "priest." So then it becomes a question of how do we understand or translate the term you're dealing with, where you have a feminine version of that—*presbytera*.

Gary Macy: The Middle Ages is a thousand years, so I mean, big differences in time there. By the way, Bill mentioned my book. A lot of these questions I really answer more fully there; it is completely comprehensible even if you're not interested in Latin or scholarship—you can just read it as a long essay. It is called *The Hidden History of Women's Ordination* and it was published by Oxford University Press in 2007.

By the Middle Ages, even in the fifth and sixth centuries, *presbyter, presbyterus, presbytera*—probably no longer means "elder." It means "priest." But, there is still a big difference in understanding exactly what the role of a priest is. I am going to give you two quick examples. Before the eleventh-century reform movement changed the definition of *ordination,* that word meant the selection by a particular community of a particular person to do a particular job for that community and only that community. If you were a bishop, you couldn't become a bishop in another place, because they didn't pick you and it's not your community. That was considered adultery; it happened, but it was really frowned on. One of the first popes who was a bishop somewhere else, after he died he was dug up, papal robes were put back on him, they chopped off his fingers, they threw him in the Tiber River. It was political, yes. It was condemned. But one of the big reasons was that he had been a bishop somewhere else and you can't do that. You were a member of the community who was picked by the community to do a job for that community. It didn't give you any power that you could take to another community.

So to be a presbyter, to be a priest in the early Middle Ages, didn't mean you could be a priest anywhere. It didn't give you that kind of power; you had a particular role to play in that community, which was to lead the liturgy for that community. But you didn't go ahead then and then move to another diocese. It was not a portable power. That only begins to appear in the thirteenth century, where theologians say that you're given the power to say Mass. Nor is there a connection particularly between the *presbyterate* and the Eucharist.

They were still debating in the middle of the twelfth century whether you *must* be a priest to consecrate the bread and wine. And at least three theologians in the twelfth century, very well-known theologians (they weren't condemned, they were quite well-respected)—Bernard and Thierry of Chartres, and then Jean Beleth—they believed and taught that the words of institution automatically consecrate, no matter who says them.

Jean Beleth has this terrific story from the seventh century about these shepherds. He says the reason we say the words of institution quietly is because we used to say them aloud, "everybody" knew them (*corpus meum*). These shepherds are having their lunch of bread and wine, and they say the words, and God strikes them dead because transubstantiation took place. So in the middle of the twelfth century, they are still deciding whether you have to be a priest to consecrate. So in those early centuries, we have a different understanding of exactly what *priest* means. You don't get a lot of powers that only you can do—you're given a job by the community, and that's one of the jobs.

And there are lots of other jobs. And all of those jobs, by the way, are called ordinations (*ordinatio*) because *ordinatio* in Latin just means "to put in order." If you put your books in alphabetical order in the early Middle Ages, it is an *ordinatio*, that's the word. So there are very different understandings of what it means to be a priest.

By the thirteenth century, all of these powers are concentrated into one person and that is a power you can take, you can't lose, forever, and you take it with you wherever you go. That is not the situation for the first

1200 years of Christianity. So that's very important when we're thinking about what priesthood is and what those words mean. And in that earlier understanding of ordination and of appointment, women played a lot bigger role. They did not understand priesthood as we understand priesthood until the thirteenth century.

Richard Miller: A follow-up question: Why did it change? Why did this notion of ordination change?

Gary Macy: I don't know if anyone knows why exactly that changed. But I will give you the reasons scholars have come up with.

The Church was very much a feudal structure by the tenth century, and that meant the dioceses were family-run institutions just like a large feudal estate would be. Lots of bishops were married, and the diocese was basically the family property. The same was true of parishes. And they were hereditary. There are good things and bad things about that.

The good things are, it's really a family structure and they have a lot more understanding of what families are about and the problems that families have. Second, it is very closely integrated into the society; it is not a separate caste of people, the clergy are part of the people, and they are picked by their own congregations. That is a strength.

A weakness is nepotism—horrible, terrible, destructive nepotism. You know, the king makes sure his brother-in-law is bishop or that his daughter is married to a bishop. For lots of different reasons, but let us just say to get some prophetic distance for the Church, they decided to remove the Church from that feudal structure. Two things they did: One, they concentrated as much power as they could into the priesthood to say priests are more powerful than lords, because lords were understood as ordained, kings were understood as ordained; this was a role in the community. So were emperors, empresses, abbots, and abbesses. So they wanted to make a very clear distinction between the power a priest or bishop had and the power a lord had. To move them that way, they said one was spiritual and one was temporal. Second, in order to destroy these hereditary parishes and dioceses, they demanded celibacy.

Now as to celibacy, I am sure most of you know, but just to be clear on that, the law from 1139 says nothing about chastity; *nothing about chastity*. It says if a priest or a deacon (and a group of other people, too, but that changed) contract a marriage, it's not valid. Now, socially that was brilliant, because not many women wanted to be in an adulterous relationship and have their children be bastards. Especially in a society that has arranged marriages: who would arrange a marriage like that? That would be suicide. But it says nothing about chastity. Celibacy is not a vow of chastity. *Celibacy* means you cannot contract a valid marriage. Well, that had the effect of giving the Church a prophetic stance over against the politics, which is extremely important and extremely powerful.

But there were downsides to it too. It meant that now priests and bishops were outside the family structure for reasons I don't think were necessary, but that is when people began to argue that women can't possibly be ordained and never were. And that has to do, again, with a number of social factors that all just seem to feed together. It wasn't inevitable, but it did in fact happen. So I think it was an attempt on the part of the Church to gain prophetic distance over the society in which they lived, something we desperately needed. On the other hand, it created a distance between the ministers and everyday life because they weren't involved directly; they became a separate caste, whereas before they had been immersed in the daily life of the community. By emphasizing the power in the priesthood as opposed to any of the other orders, they created a kind of clericalism. That wasn't their intent, but they created the possibilities for clericalism. It wasn't inevitable, and again, how that evolved did not affect women well.

Richard Miller: There are many questions around this issue. Let me push one more here. Were the abbesses able to consecrate bread and wine into the Body and Blood of Christ?

Gary Macy: I think they would not have understood it that way. They certainly always believed that the Risen Christ was present in the Body and Blood, but working out the technicalities of that—how that is possible—transubstantiation is one way of saying how it's possible for the Real Presence to be there. Real Presence and transubstantiation are quite different. Transubstantiation is one attempt to say how it's possible for there to be a Real Presence. But it's not until the twelfth century that theologians are working out what is necessary for the Real Presence. Does it have to be a priest? Does it have to be the words of consecration? Some theologians in the twelfth century speculated that it was the Sign of the Cross that made the Real Presence. In fact, they argued, and they weren't right about this, that originally the only prayer that anyone said at Mass was the Our Father because it is the only prayer Jesus gave us; the rest was all made up. So there seem to have been communities that used the Our Father to consecrate—the Waldensians, for instance, because they were going back to what they thought was an older tradition.

They thought it came from Gregory the Great. They misread Gregory and that's what they thought.

In the middle of the twelfth century they are still deciding how exactly this all works, so to go to centuries before the twelfth century and say did they think transubstantiation took place...well, they wouldn't have been thinking that way at all. Did they think the Real Presence was there? Yes. They would have thought there was a Real Presence. That's about the best I can say, because I'm reading back into the past. Now, theologically you can do that. I must say, very quickly, historians—we can't do that. We're not allowed to do that. But theologically you could say, "But was that real?"

Richard Miller: Mary Ann, you mentioned in your talk briefly at the very end that Mary often filled in what is missing in the Tradition. Could you give some examples and expound on that a little bit, please?

Mary Ann Zimmer: One good example would be that grain-goddess image that we saw at the very beginning. As Europe became Christianized, they were supposed to give up the idols of their past. So as the Christian God came in, and there was a dilemma for ordinary farmers because this power they had appealed to for success with their crops—there was no longer a power who took an interest at that level. So the role that Mary started to play was as the grain goddess had been, concerned about their day-to-day survival, the survival of their crops. They attributed to Mary that kind of power. It seems that God was more distant from their daily concerns, and so Mary was considered more approachable; it would be more likely that *she* would be concerned about a person at that level. And that kind of supposition, I think, has gone on in many, many devotions to Mary of various kinds.

Eileen Burke-Sullivan: Another area of that, Yves Congar in the 1950s wrote a very, very interesting essay in which he talks about the lack of the conscious presence of the Holy Spirit in the Latin Church from the eleventh century. The Eastern and Western Churches split, and he maintained that the role of the Spirit was subsumed by Mary, who took on all the titles of the Holy Spirit: Comforter of the Afflicted, Consoler, and so forth; and, by the Real Presence in the Eucharist and by infallibility in the Pope so that the functions of the Holy Spirit were subsumed in those three roles as it were. So Mary replaced the Holy Spirit in the kind of intimacy and in some respects in the salvific acts— the transformation, the salvific acts.

Mary Ann Zimmer: One of the things Elizabeth Johnson talks about in her book is that she thinks it would be more accurate and more profitable for us to stop thinking of Mary as semi-God and think of her more as a disciple who accompanies us in our discipleship. But I think one of the problems with that is that as long as the symbol system for God is controlled by a male presence—and a celibate male presence—there is still going to be on some deep level that perceived missing element in our understanding of God. So I don't think we can sort of separate Mary out of all of that by force of will. I think there is something too deep going on.

Richard Miller: Gary, at the end of your talk you suggested that if women had greater powers in the first 1200 years than they do now, that raises the question about women in the future. How does your history relate to the role of women in the Church's future?

Gary Macy: This difference in the understanding of ordination, that's not any research I did at all. It was all done a long time ago by Yves Congar. He's the guy. I mean, he and two other of his Dominican colleagues, Pierre-Marie Gy and Pierre Benoît, did all of this wonderful research showing how the definition of ordination changed. They laid that out very clearly. And it's in the earlier definition of *ordination* they'll use for the selection, and these are Congar's words, "for the selection and appointment by the community from someone in the community to a particular vocation or role in the community." That is the earlier understanding of ordination. It's in that system that women could play a greater role. This is what I think history is offering us the opportunity to contemplate: If we've had different structures at different times in the history of the Church, that means that the structure we have now is not inevitable. It's not the only one that God can imagine or that the Spirit can imagine, because we've had others. And so we can have others again. The teaching of history is freedom from the tyranny of the present. The present is not inevitable.

So, I look around and I see, we just don't have priests. They are disappearing. Even the Vatican in its very optimistic (probably too optimistic) statement a couple of years ago admitted that there are the same number of priests in the world now as in 1971, and the population of the world has doubled. That's in the *world*. I don't have to tell you about the priest shortage here in the United States.

So what's happening? As one of our speakers said, 80 percent of the people who do ministry in parishes and dioceses are laypeople. And where do those laypeople come from? They come from communities that choose them to play a particular role or vocation in their community. So slowly, I think, by default but gratuitously in the fullest sense of the word *grace*, we're going back to a model that's similar to those early centuries. And there's nothing wrong with that. It's very slowly turning out that those are the people who are actually doing the majority of the jobs. One of the things I see happening on the West Coast, but I also know it's happening in the Midwest, is there are more and more pastoral associates picked by their communities, appointed by the bishop. They hold the liturgy every Sunday, in many cases they do the marriages, they do the baptisms. I understand now there are over three thousand of them in the United States. Well, wouldn't that be nice—this is me speaking, please take it for what it's worth—wouldn't it be nice if we experimented with that tradition? If we actually had people coming out of our communities that were part of our communities? Now some of them are married and some of them are not married. Some of them are women and some of them are not women. But they're the people the community picks to be their leaders. That would be drawing on a very, very old and original tradition in the Church. And I think very creative things could be done with that. And that would allow, of course, women a much larger role because it wouldn't matter if you were a man or a woman as it doesn't matter for pastoral associates. So that's one possibility.

I also should add that this is a much older tradition than you would think. According to a very interesting little study that is hard to get your hands on about bishops that was done by Garrett Sweeney in England years ago—he was a canon and master of St. Edmund's House, the Catholic College at Cambridge—he did a study on how bishops were chosen. The very first time that the papacy ever even claimed the right, *even claimed the right*, to appoint all of the bishops in the world, was 1899 in a treaty with Guatemala! I mean, there's no tradition in Catholicism until the very end of the nineteenth century for the papacy to appoint bishops. The law from 1179, which was in effect until 1917, was that bishops are chosen by the priests of their dioceses with the consent of their people, which goes back to the second century! And as a historian I just go ballistic because when they changed the law in 1917 they changed the law on the basis of nothing! Of no tradition! We don't have that tradition! Excuse me; I get a little worked up about this one. So that is not old, that's very, very new. That's *very, very* new.

William Harmless: Before we go to the consent of the people, I've got a warning story. I work on Saint Augustine. Here's how Saint Augustine became a priest, or presbyter: He happened to go to Church one day in Hippo. The bishop stands up in front of everybody and says, "Ladies and gentlemen, we need a new presbyter for our Church. I'd like you to nominate somebody." Everybody looked around, they saw this guy who used to be an orator up with the Emperor in Milan who had kind of been writing some good pamphlets, they grabbed him, dragged him to the front of the Church and he was ordained on the spot! Weeping! He says later why he was weeping, but the locals thought he's weeping because he doesn't get to be bishop. I think he was probably weeping because he lost his freedom. Remember, he was there for life, so there are little hazards in this proposal here. You know, the early Church had very good clergy, but you can see how they got the job. There was nothing like seminaries and nothing like claiming you had a vocation; and so you got it forced into you. You could tell the story of Anselm of Canterbury and how he was made the bishop of Canterbury. Forced ordination was a common thing, so let's weigh this carefully before we go this route.

Gary Macy: Well, history never exactly repeats itself. We can learn. We can refine that. But that's very true. By the way, you didn't have to be a priest before you were a bishop, not even if you were pope. Priests became bishops, but there were deacons who became bishops, too, and they didn't ordain them priests in the meantime—they were deacons one day and bishops the next because there were just two roles in the community. There was nothing sort of magic about the priesthood. Interestingly enough, as far as I know, the first pope who insisted that he be ordained a priest—he was deacon, chosen as pope, elected as pope—was Pope Gregory VII, the man for whom the Gregorian reforms are named. Before that, they didn't bother with that. It's just a different system. But yes, we really have to refine that system. There were big problems with that system, and that's why they changed it. Knowing this history, however, free us up to envision other possible structures.

Richard Miller: This is for the whole panel: What possibility (or possibilities) do you discern, perceive, envision for the future of women in the Church?

Eileen Burke-Sullivan: At the present time, it's very interesting. I'm involved in formation of these lay ministers that Gary's talking about, and just recently the American bishops have promulgated a document that requires formal education at the master's level for these folks, so in other words there's a kind of recognition similar to the decrees of Trent—that whoever does this kind of ministry ought to be educated for it or formed for it. My own sense is that we're in a period of radical change, I mean dramatic change, on all levels: the computer, the Internet, the communication systems, the forms of education, all kinds of things are rapidly changing. It's not surprising in the context of this that there's a great deal of violence, because violence always accompanies change. People get frightened. So then you take absolutist stands. My experience of looking at Church history, and particularly in liturgy, is that every time we get really absolute, it's like somebody that's seeing a therapist and doesn't want to deal with their dark side, they go into resistance. Well I think that when we get absolutists in all kinds of ways that we are at a breaking point of some kind. What that breaking point means sociologically is different than what it means for an individual person, but when there's that quality of resistance, the shift occurs relatively quickly, and then the community of faith will say, "As we have always universally taught and done, thus and such is what God desires." So it's kind of a time that we look around and we try and discern what is happening, what directions are already occurring, and then look to see what choices the Spirit is inviting us to make. And there will be suffering. There will be difficulty. There will be a shift. There will be refinement. But what is now is clearly not working as well as some people would fantasize that it ought to, we're in the midst of change.

Mary Ann Zimmer: I have something that I envision happening and also something that I fear. One is what Bernard Lee talks about when he talks about the growing lay hermeneutic in the Church, meaning that as more and more laypeople are getting theological education and acting in professional and academic roles, the way we interpret theology is going to change because those people have different experience than if all of your theologians are clergy, and that leaves room for new creativity and new insight.

The thing I'm kind of concerned about is that that's still a professionalized role and as ecclesial ministers, lay ministers become more and more professionalized. That becomes a professional role, and what I'm concerned about is not that I don't think there should be lay ministers or that I think that's not a good thing, but what happens is we're still dealing with a double layer where there are these professional Christians or Catholics and then there's everybody else, and at what point do we get real about Vatican II's statement that the role of the laity is to Christianize the secular world or to redeem the secular world? When do we focus on that? The people who are not professional Church people, and what happens in their work life, in their home life, in their soccer practice, and their struggle to be married and all of that? You know, when do we get seriously concerned about that? So that's my concern.

William Harmless: A concept I found helpful is by a liturgical theologian named David Power. He wrote a book called *Ministries Institutionalized and Uninstitutionalized*, and I think that is the better category. It is commonplace, we often talk about lay ministry. For me, to my ear, that's a contradiction in terms. If you are a full-time professional minister to the Christian community, you are clergy. Now you may not have the whole canon law that protects you and is associated with priesthood or with bishops or with deacons, but if you are doing it full time, if you look at what has happened in the last fifty years, sitting on this panel, the number of women who are teaching theology with PhDs at university levels as full-time professionals who may not be institutionalized with a Church service—that is full-time professional ministry to the Church.

And different ministries have trajectories. Something that may not be ordained now, to use that earlier medieval language, might be in a hundred years. And so it is uninstitutionalized ministry that may not be currently ordained but might be in the future. The issue that Mary Ann raises is the crucial one, which is the larger issue of the Christian community to evangelize the world and to do the justice of God. One of the risks of the language of lay ministry is that we can confuse the service interior to the community (which is ministry) to the larger exterior mission, and it's urgent that we be doing both.

And also the problem is recognizing that this stuff is moving. I mean, if you study the history of ministry, one of the great inventions, and for all the risks of the clericalization that happened in the Middle Ages, one of the popes who helped do this was Pope Innocent III, who was a great reformer, who absorbed a vision, a pastoral reform, from his education at the University of Paris. He put his blessing on two newfangled religious groups called the Franciscans and the Dominicans, who revolutionized ministry and were incredibly controversial in their own time. I come from another equally controversial ministry that wasn't clearly regulated initially, namely the Jesuits. We had a view of what you do as priest. If you look at what a sixteenth-century priest did, Ignatius of Loyola didn't let us do any of those things. In other words, Ignatius's vision of priesthood didn't match what the sixteenth century thought about priests. Ignatius's imagination was focused on being an apostle.

So the study of the history of ministry is a study of change. And to look at it and watch that, even when the same words are used, you might not have the same realities, or you may have brand new realities without a change in vocabulary, so we have to be very alert to the issues of what is going on actually in the practice on the ground.

Susan Calef: Well, I think my own feeling at this time is I look at the Church that I've been a part of for these fifty-some-odd years. I'm trying desperately to have hope, and that's why I said to you I'm very gratified by this particular event, although certainly the restrictions, or the inability of the Church to truly use all of the gifts of women grieves me deeply. There are so many gifts that are needed desperately by our people. And they are available. Many women have those gifts. Many men who were formerly priests have them. So there is tremendous heartache and loss and need in our Church, and that really grieves me.

I also worry—I work with young people and I go to Churches both Catholic and Protestant to do this kind of adult education, and what is clear to me is that all of the Churches are graying, looking like this. And I do worry as I listen to young people. Are they going to be with us? Who are we going to be ministering to? And on the one hand, that also connects with my other grief, because I think women bring a lot of creativity and they look at relationships. I mean there is a lot of creative work that needs to be done for the sake of keeping this Church afloat. Eileen used the word *suffering.* I guess my own feeling is that the Church as we know it is dying. I think we're into the Paschal Mystery. I feel we're deeply in Paschal Mystery. And right now we're in the Passion and the dying. That's my read of it.

But, you know, we were talking at lunch and I said I often feel that at 50 it is interesting to discover you've booked passage on the Titanic is the metaphor I use. And you know, I can laugh about it but it's also painful. But partly because we are in such denial, I feel as if leadership is often in denial about the iceberg dead ahead. So I feel like some of us are desperately trying to minister…in fact, one of the priests describes priestly ministry as hospice care right now. Interesting metaphor. As I say, I think of myself as over here in the edge, trying to get people into lifeboats. So I think there is great frustration. I know there's great frustration among women and many laymen about what they see needs to happen, but because we don't have the voice in the governance, we can't do what we feel needs to be done. So I guess I really struggle to have hope.

Young people in many ways give me hope, but I see them increasingly not finding the Spirit in the Church, and they are leaving us. And that grieves me, because there are so many gifts that I think if we tapped them could be actually creating a much more vibrant community with immense creativity to draw others in and then to give us, as Bill was talking about, that wonderful power of the Good News to go forth and evangelize the world. So these days I'm not even focusing on involving women because my feeling is "add women and stir" to the Church is not going to fix it. I think we can do some things a whole lot better by adding women, but I think we have much bigger issues about looking at governance and our structures, which is what we have been talking about. I think the structures we have need to change, as Gary's been saying, and we need to find something else that is much more community based so that there's accountability between our leaders and ourselves, and we can really be a spirited community because then there would be life. Sorry not to have better news.

Richard Miller: We have one last question: How can we liberate the relational character of the Trinity from its androcentric expression—Father, Son, Spirit?

Susan Calef: We need to do more of this kind of theological education. We need to help people think about God language and free it up. Father, Son, and Spirit language is fine, it's traditional. But it's not enough. And as I say, many, many women that I know are increasingly wandering away from the Church, and more of the young people talk about being on a spiritual path and searching for God. Part of it is, and that's what Mary Ann was talking about with the Mary issue, people are hungering also for what would be thought of in a sense as that maternal aspect, and there's an instinct that there is the feminine face of God, but it's still not a part of our liturgical practice, it's not a part of our prayer life unless we're gathering in special arenas where everybody is OK with that, so that is one thing I think has to happen.

Eileen Burke-Sullivan: It strikes me that one of the things we can't do is lose the personal character of the Godhead, the trinitarian persons. So I understand the Church's reluctance to accept Creator, Sanctifier, and so on. I think the personhood of relationality is terribly important in the nature. It strikes me that we have to do a whole lot more to think about the core relationality of the Trinity theologically, I mean, there is a lot of "communal" work being done, a lot of Communion theology trying to be done around this and the Trinity as the primary sign of community is crucial. I think as long as the institutional Church remains profoundly hierarchical rather than communal in a sense of much more intimate relationality, that is a hard distinction, that problem is going to be there.

I would like to suggest that the feminine voice or the feminine face of God historically has always been the Church. Mother Church is supposed to be the feminine face of God. And at this particular moment, when not only is the Godhead being defined in masculine terms but the Church, too, that becomes very problematic, I think. So it really does strike me that we are in this cauldron, if you will, of change, and it's really important to stay with the transformational process and not become impatient or unwilling to be faithful to the process of growth and change that we're being called to. Those who have that insight or that desire have a charism, therefore, to be willing to work with that desire. The more we can build community with each other, the more we can authentically pray and share faith with each other in meaningful ways as adults, the more I think we can illuminate the truth about the Trinity and witness it as Church and maybe the institutional structures will catch up.

William Harmless: I have to say the question bothers me because I think we've got it right and I really think the Trinitarian language is correct. And I have studied this, we would need a least a day of this length to take you through how the Church came to that decision. It is a brilliant, brilliant, careful, thoughtful, profound decision full of the recognition of mystery, and anyone wanting to move away from the traditional language of Father, Son, and Spirit, three persons in one Essence, does not understand the stakes, and I think we have to guard that with great care.

Mary Ann Zimmer: I think I would go with Eileen, that the last word is that God is in charge of the process, and we need to follow God. I learned a lot from belonging to a congregation that had a motherhouse behind the Iron Curtain because we have as part of our heritage the stories of how you act when people tell you what you can't do, and the answer is you do it. So not to be intimidated by the realities that we face, but to be faithful to the vision that we have and to make that a vision we share with each other whether the institution entirely shares that or not. And I don't mean that in some kind of wild, irresponsible, go off and dump the Tradition. Obviously that's not what *I'm* doing. But I think there is a way not to spend all of our time grieving. Grieving is a healthy thing when there's a lot to grieve, but there's also a great richness, and the Spirit hasn't abandoned us, so I think we need to attend to that and encourage one another in that. On the days that I can't remember that, I want somebody else to remember it for me. On the days *you* can't remember it, I'll try to remember it for you.

Richard Miller: I would like to thank the University of Saint Mary for sponsoring this event along with Rockhurst University. I would also like to thank everyone for spending the whole day with us and for all your work in the Church and all your various ministries. And I would very much like to thank the speakers for their ministry of theology and history.

Speakers' Biographies

Richard W. Miller, PhD

Richard Miller is Assistant Professor of Systematic Theology at Creighton University. He began his academic career at the University of Notre Dame with a BA in theology and philosophy, and then received an MA and PhD in systematic theology from Boston College. His scholarly interests include the problem of reconciling the Christian doctrine of providence with evil and human suffering, the notion of God as Mystery, the implications of the doctrine of the Trinity for ontology, and the thought of Karl Rahner and Thomas Aquinas as resources for contemporary theology. He is one of the founders of the this lecture series and has been a contributor to and editor of the published version of this series: *We Hold These Truths: Catholicism and American Political Life* (2008), *Prayer in the Catholic Tradition* (2007), *Spirituality for the 21st Century: Experiencing God in the Catholic Tradition* (2006), and *Lay Ministry in the Catholic Church: Visioning Church Ministry Through the Wisdom of the Past* (2005). He also contributed to *The Catholic Church in the 21st Century: Finding Hope for its Future in the Wisdom of Its Past* (2004).

Susan A. Calef, PhD

Susan A. Calef is Assistant Professor of Theology and Director of Graduate Studies in Theology at Creighton University, where she also teaches in the Christian Spirituality Program. Dr. Calef earned an MA in biblical literature and languages from Catholic Theological Union, Chicago, which included studies in Greece, Turkey, Israel, and Egypt; and later an MA and PhD in New Testament and Christian origins from the University of Notre Dame, where she studied in the Christianity and Judaism in Antiquity program. Much of Dr. Calef's research has focused on canonical and extracanonical texts that depict women or that bear upon the lives of women. Her publications include several articles in collections: "Prayer in the New Testament," "Thecla: 'Tried and True' and the Inversion of Romance," "The Shape of Family and Family Values: 'The Bible Tells Us So,' or Does It?", "The Radicalism of Jesus the Prophet: Implications for Christian Family," and "By Grit and Grace: Women on the Early Christian Frontier." She is currently finishing a book entitled *Willing Spirit, Weak Flesh: Mark's Spirituality of Discipleship* and is drafting a second book on the narrative theology and spirituality of the four Gospels tentatively titled *Gospel Questions, Gospel Quest.* Due to the growing interest in biblical education and the many requests that she receives to speak to adult audiences, she has initiated an educational-outreach project, DiaLogos Presentations, which produces audio CDs and supplementary materials on biblical topics.

William Harmless, SJ, PhD

William Harmless is Professor of Theology at Creighton University in Omaha, Nebraska. He is a native of Kansas City and graduated from Rockhurst High School. He has been a member of the Society of Jesus since 1978 and received his doctorate from Boston College in 1990. His specialty is the history and theology of early Christianity. One focus of his research has been Saint Augustine of Hippo (354–430). His first book was *Augustine and the Catechumenate*, published by Liturgical Press in 1995. His latest project is the soon-to-be completed *St. Augustine: A Reader*, to be published by Catholic University of America Press in 2009. A second area of research is early Christian monasticism, especially the fourth-century and fifth-century desert fathers of Egypt. In 2004, Oxford University Press published his large-scale study, *Desert Christians: An Introduction to the Literature of Early Monasticism*. He recently served as editor for the English edition of a new reference book, Hubertus Drobner's *The Fathers of the Church: A Comprehensive Introduction* (Hendrickson, 2007). His latest book is *Mystics*, published in 2007 by Oxford University Press.

Gary Macy, PhD

Dr. Gary Macy, The John Nobili, SJ, Professor of Theology at Santa Clara University, received his bachelor's and master's degrees from Marquette University, where he specialized in historical and sacramental theology. He earned his doctoral degree in divinity from Cambridge University in 1978. He has published several books on the history of the Eucharist and collaborated with Dr. Bernard Cooke on a two-volume series on the history of ordination and women for Scarecrow Press. In 2006, Dr. Macy collaborated with Dr. Orlando Espín to edit the second in a series of books from the Center for the Study of Latino/a Catholicism at the University of San Diego entitled *The Future Of Our Past: Explorations In the Theology Of Tradition* (Orbis Books). Dr. Macy's most recent book, *The Hidden History of Women's Ordination: Female Clergy in the Medieval West*, appeared from Oxford University Press in 2007. Dr. Macy has published over twenty articles. In 1991–1992, Dr. Macy was Heroditus Fellow at the Institute for Advanced Study in Princeton; during the 2005-2006 academic year, he was awarded the Senior Luce Fellowship at the National Humanities Center in North Carolina. He has won three national awards for his books and articles.

Eileen Burke-Sullivan, STD

Dr. Burke is Assistant Professor of Theology and the Director of the Master of Arts in Ministry program at Creighton University in Omaha. Eileen received her BA degree in English and music at St. Mary College in Leavenworth, KS, completed master's degrees in music at the University of Colorado in Boulder and theology at Creighton, a licentiate in sacred theology, and a doctorate in sacred theology at Weston Jesuit School of Theology in Cambridge, MA. She specialized in systematic theology with an emphasis in ecclesiology. She holds subspecialties in liturgy and spirituality. She is coauthoring a volume on Ignatian spirituality with her brother, Kevin Burke, SJ, and is editing a collection of essays in Christian spirituality. Dr. Burke served as adjunct faculty for the Creighton spirituality program for a number of summers, taught at Weston Jesuit during her last two years there, and also taught at the University of Dallas in its graduate lay-ministry program while serving full time as a lay ecclesial minister of the Catholic Church in both parish and diocesan positions.

Robert Ellsberg

Robert Ellsberg is the publisher and editor in chief of Orbis Books, the publishing arm of the Maryknoll Fathers. In the late 1970s he worked for five years with Dorothy Day at the Catholic Worker in New York City. After her death in 1980, he edited *Dorothy Day: Selected Writings*. Before coming to work at Orbis in 1987, he studied theology at Harvard Divinity School. He has edited anthologies of writings by Flannery O'Connor, Mohandas Gandhi, Charles de Foucauld, and Thich Nhat Hanh. He is the author of *All Saints: Daily Reflections on Saints, Prophets, and Witnesses for Our Time* (recently included in *One Hundred Great Catholic Books*), *The Saints' Guide to Happiness,* and *Blessed Among All Women,* which won three Catholic Press Association Book Awards. His most recent book is *The Duty of Delight: The Diaries of Dorothy Day.* He lives with his family in Ossining, New York.

Mary Ann Zimmer, ND, PhD

Dr. Zimmer, a Notre Dame Sister of Omaha, Nebraska, is currently Assistant Professor of Religious Studies at Marywood University in Scranton, Pennsylvania. She has her BA in theology from Creighton University, her MDiv from Weston Jesuit School of Theology, and her PhD in theological studies from Emory University. Her work has appeared in the *Proceedings of the Forum on Religion and Public Life*, in *In the Embrace of God: A Feminist Reader in Theological Anthropology,* and in the journal *Liturgy.*